Deterrence, Diplomacy and the Risk of Conflict Over Taiwan

Bill Emmott

'Bill Emmott has done a masterly job of highlighting the necessity of a sophisticated and comprehensive deterrence strategy in the Indo-Pacific given the real dangers of Chinese military coercion against Taiwan. His work is particularly profound in warning that we have downplayed the taboo topic of nuclear escalation in a Taiwan Strait crisis even though a US–China conflict would be the first in history between nuclear great powers.'

– *Dennis Wilder, former Deputy Assistant Director for East Asia and the Pacific, CIA (2015–16); Assistant Professor of the Practice and Senior Fellow for the Initiative for US–China Dialogue on Global Issues, Georgetown University*

'Bill Emmott is correct to describe our task as making war over Taiwan "inevitably catastrophic and therefore inconceivable". Japan both can and is determined to contribute to this goal by strengthening regional deterrence efforts.'

– *Ishii Masafumi, former Director for Policy Planning, Ministry of Foreign Affairs, Japan; former Japanese Ambassador to Indonesia*

Deterrence, Diplomacy and the Risk of Conflict Over Taiwan

Bill Emmott

IISS The International Institute for Strategic Studies

The International Institute for Strategic Studies
Arundel House | 6 Temple Place | London | WC2R 2PG | UK

First published July 2024 by **Routledge**
4 Park Square, Milton Park, Abingdon, Oxon, OX14 4RN

for **The International Institute for Strategic Studies**
Arundel House, 6 Temple Place, London, WC2R 2PG, UK
www.iiss.org

Simultaneously published in the USA and Canada by **Routledge**
52 Vanderbilt Avenue, New York, NY 10017

Routledge is an imprint of Taylor & Francis, an Informa Business

© 2024 The International Institute for Strategic Studies

DIRECTOR-GENERAL AND CHIEF EXECUTIVE Dr Bastian Giegerich
SERIES EDITOR Dr Benjamin Rhode
ASSOCIATE EDITOR Alice Aveson
EDITORIAL Gregory Brooks, Christopher Harder, Jill Lally, Michael Marsden
PRODUCTION Alessandra Beluffi, Ravi Gopar, Jade Panganiban, James Parker, Kelly Verity
COVER ARTWORK ChatGPT-4 by OpenAI and Jade Panganiban

The International Institute for Strategic Studies is an independent centre for research, information and debate on the problems of conflict, however caused, that have, or potentially have, an important military content. The Council and Staff of the Institute are international and its membership is drawn from almost 100 countries. The Institute is independent and it alone decides what activities to conduct. It owes no allegiance to any government, any group of governments or any political or other organisation. The IISS stresses rigorous research with a forward-looking policy orientation and places particular emphasis on bringing new perspectives to the strategic debate.

The Institute's publications are designed to meet the needs of a wider audience than its own membership and are available on subscription, by mail order and in good bookshops. Further details at www.iiss.org.

All rights reserved. No part of this book may be reprinted or reproduced or utilised in any form or by any electronic, mechanical or other means, now known or hereafter invented, including photocopying and recording, or in any information storage or retrieval system, without permission in writing from the publishers.

British Library Cataloguing in Publication Data
A catalogue record for this book is available from the British Library

Library of Congress Cataloging in Publication Data

ADELPHI series
ISSN 1944-5571

ADELPHI AP508–510
ISBN 978-1-032-89633-5 / eB 978-1-003-54382-4

Contents

	Author	6
	Acknowledgements	7
	Map of Taiwan and its surrounding region	8
	Introduction: Danger, hiding in plain sight	9
Chapter One	**Why Indo-Pacific deterrence matters**	19
	Why the stakes in Taiwan are so high 22	
	The conflict to be deterred 35	
Chapter Two	**Deterrence lessons from Ukraine**	37
	Eight lessons from Ukraine 37	
	Specific implications for China 45	
	Specific implications for Taiwan 47	
	Specific implications for the United States 48	
Chapter Three	**Yardsticks for deterrence**	51
	A world in flux 52	
	Rationality without MADness 54	
	An unstable status quo 55	
	Yardsticks for Indo-Pacific deterrence 56	
Chapter Four	**Consistent America, inconstant America**	59
	Political will: consistency and clarity of deterrence messages 62	
	Military capability and coalition credibility 65	
	The narrative yardstick 72	
Chapter Five	**Taiwan and its predicament**	79
	Military resilience 86	
	Civil resilience 91	
	Narrative clarity 95	
Chapter Six	**Coercive China, deterrent China**	99
	Deterring an intervention 104	
	Controlling the nuclear risk 106	
	Controlling the narrative 110	
Chapter Seven	**Allies and partners: the role of Japan**	115
	Japan, from self-defence to constrained deterrence 118	
	Constrained but speedy? 124	
	Many unanswered questions 127	
Chapter Eight	**The Philippines, Australia and other partners**	133
	The Philippines as an unsinkable logistics centre 135	
	Australia: far away but now committed 138	
	Other allies and bystanders, near and far 142	
	ASEAN non-centrality 144	
	Limits to the ASEAN way 147	
	Dreaming of a more balanced region 149	
	Conclusion: Nostalgic for Cold War realism	153
	Needed: the good aspect of Cold War diplomacy 156	
	Notes	163
	Index	183

AUTHOR

Bill Emmott is Chairman of the IISS Trustees and an independent writer and consultant. He spent 26 years at *The Economist*, which he joined in 1980, working as a correspondent and editor in Brussels, Tokyo and London, on subjects ranging from politics to finance, economics and business. In 1993, he was appointed editor-in-chief, a post he held for 13 years before stepping down in 2006.

He holds honorary degrees from Warwick, City and Northwestern universities, and is an honorary fellow of Magdalen College, Oxford. He is Chair of the Japan Society of the UK, an Ushioda Fellow of Tokyo College, University of Tokyo, Chair of the International Trade Institute, a trustee of the Chester Beatty Library, a Senior Adviser for Montrose Associates, and is a member of the Comitato Scientifico of the Centro Einaudi in Turin. He writes for *La Stampa* in Italy, *Nikkei Business* and the *Mainichi Shimbun* in Japan, and occasionally for the *Financial Times*. He is the author of numerous books on Japan, Asia, Italy and the West, his previous one being *Japan's Far More Female Future: Increasing Gender Equality and Reducing Workplace Insecurity Will Make Japan Stronger* (Oxford University Press, 2020).

ACKNOWLEDGEMENTS

At the IISS, I am especially grateful to Benjamin Rhode, the Editor of the *Adelphi* series, for having encouraged me to write this volume and for his very helpful input and editing throughout the process. Other former and current IISS colleagues who have been particularly helpful with critical input and connections include James Crabtree, James Hackett, Henry Boyd, Robert Ward, Karl Dewey, Meia Nouwens, Veerle Nouwens, Aaron Connelly, Evan Laksmana, Yuka Koshino, Leigh Morris Sloane, Mina Konishi and last but not least, Bastian Giegerich. In the editorial team, I thank Alice Aveson for her copy-editing and scrupulous attention to detail while she shepherded the book through to production, and Jade Panganiban for her work on the graphics. Many experts have provided me with invaluable guidance, often on a non-attributable basis, but I would particularly like to thank Sir Lawrence Freedman for reading and commenting on an early draft, and Richard Bush for setting me off in a good direction on Taiwan. My annual public lecture in July 2023 as an Ushioda Fellow at Tokyo College, University of Tokyo, provided an excellent first opportunity to explore some of the themes of this book.

Map 1: **Taiwan and its surrounding region**

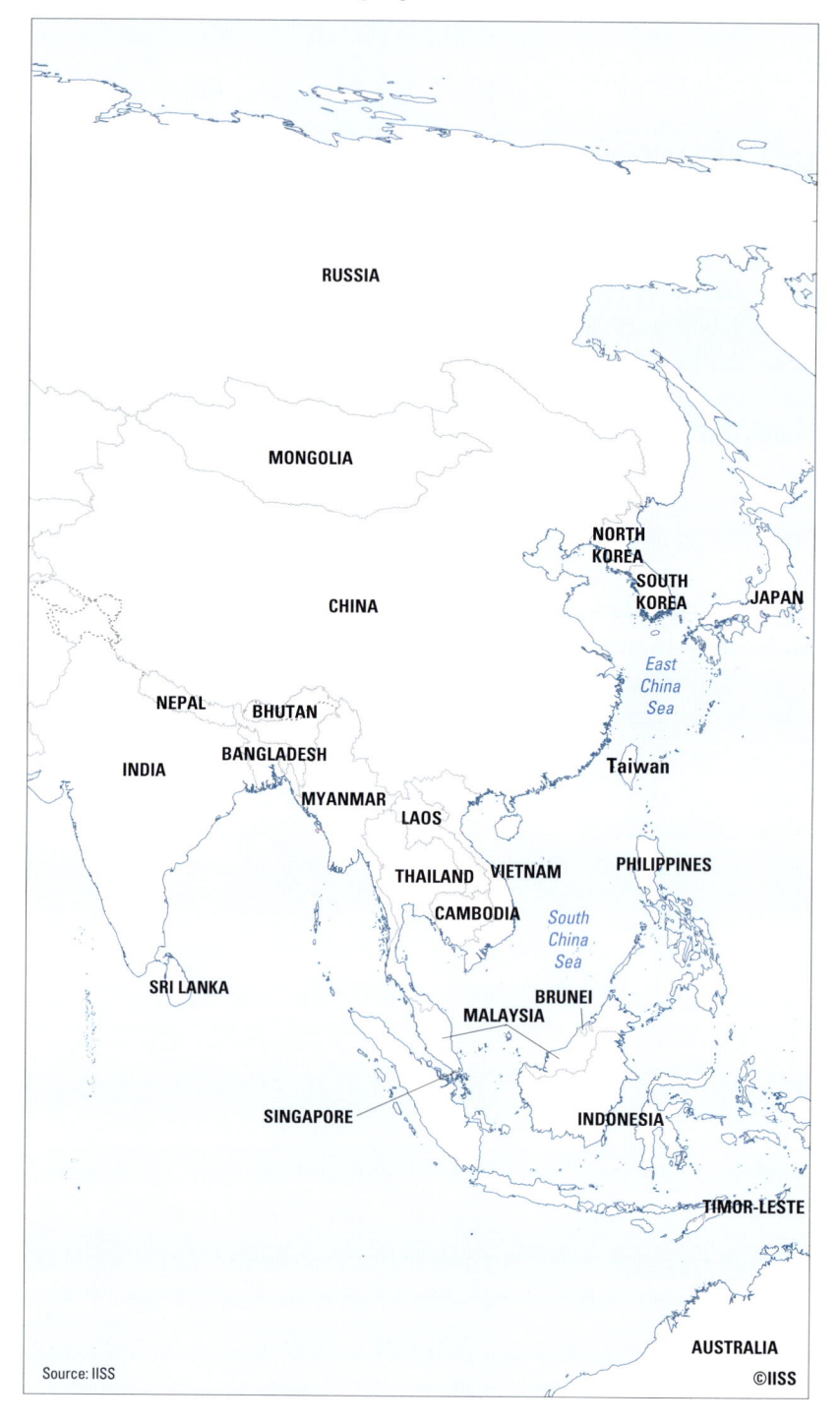

INTRODUCTION

Danger, hiding in plain sight

We are all deterrers now. But are we really serious about it in the Indo-Pacific, the place where it matters most? Have we truly appreciated what deterrence entails and what is at issue? The suspicion that gave rise to this *Adelphi* book is that the answer to the first question may be 'yes', but the answer to the second is 'only in part'.

Having been a central element of strategy during the Cold War, deterrence faded from prominence during the first decade of the twenty-first century when non-state actors and rogue states rather than nuclear superpowers became the West's principal adversaries, and a desire to replace deterrence with pre-emption took hold, primarily in the United States.[1] To call the 1990s a 'unipolar moment' was an exaggeration tinged with some hubris, but it did capture the fact that a third world war was no longer a serious threat and that the US enjoyed overwhelming military predominance, making deterrence in its by-then traditional, nuclear form less relevant.[2]

Whatever it should be called, that moment is over. The revival of great-power competition has brought the prospect of global conflict, and with it a focus on deterrence, back to centre stage. Yet in its first big test, Russia's invasion of Ukraine, deterrence failed. One could argue that it was never really tried: after all, Russia had received only minor punishments after its annexation of Crimea in 2014. International life continued fairly normally for Russia, and it even hosted the FIFA World Cup in 2018. Nonetheless, plenty of efforts were made to discourage it from invading its neighbour, including economic engagement, diplomatic reassurance and warnings.

As we now know, whether one terms it deterrence, compellence or just coercive diplomacy, none of that discouragement worked and Russia went ahead in February 2022. It was not deterred by any fear of sanctions or isolation, nor by being told that it would thereby be breaking international law and the United Nations Charter, nor by evidence of the reach and quality of American intelligence-gathering. Nor was it deterred by the possibility that the West would respond to an invasion by expanding the training and provision of weapons to Ukraine in which Western countries had already been engaged since 2014. It is now clear that in the absence of any declared willingness by NATO forces to intervene, only a belief that Ukraine's resistance would be strong and perhaps inflict serious costs would have been capable of deterring what was evidently a determined invader, and that President Vladimir Putin appears to have expected his forces to prevail in a matter of days. That view was buttressed by Russia's willingness to threaten the use of nuclear weapons as a means to ensure that NATO leaders did not change their minds. Moreover, it is conventional to say that deterrence must come with reassurance, and yet all efforts at the diplomatic assurance of Putin that Russia's security was not under threat also failed, perhaps having been doomed from the outset.

In fact, the biggest diplomatic assurance that Putin received acted as an encouragement, as it was an assurance from a 'strategic partner' that their two countries had shared goals in international affairs. It came three weeks before his invasion when, in Beijing on 4 February 2022, Putin and China's President Xi Jinping signed a lengthy Joint Statement saying among many other things that Russia and China would 'stand against attempts by external forces to undermine security and stability in their common adjacent regions [and] intend to counter interference by outside forces in the internal affairs of sovereign countries under any pretext'.[3]

That declaration made it clear that Russia and China consider it their right to have spheres of influence around their borders, and to follow their own definitions of 'security and stability', while themselves interfering in other sovereign countries should they see fit.

Such a statement was itself intended to have a deterrent effect, in this case chiefly on the West through the clear inference that two of the world's three strongest nuclear powers were now acting in concert. It simultaneously served as a rallying cry to other countries that might wish to resist Western leadership or Western interpretations of international law and might like Chinese or Russian support in doing so. The challenge that any Western strategy would need to counter had thereby been magnified, even if this Russo-Chinese strategic partnership that knows 'no limits', according to the Joint Statement, has not yet taken the form of a military alliance.[4]

Thanks to that magnified challenge, deterrence – whether adjectivally enhanced as being 'extended deterrence' to protect allies under America's nuclear umbrella or more newly as 'integrated deterrence' connecting multiple domains as well as multiple partners – is now the name of the game in US and wider Western policy in the Indo-Pacific.[5] To put it brutally, deterrence failed in Europe, so it had better be employed more effectively around the Asian danger spots of Taiwan and North Korea.

The reasons for this are simple and stark. The first is that, as the Russo-Chinese strategic partnership makes clear, there are no neat regional boundaries or delineations where great-power competition is involved. As Japan's Prime Minister Kishida Fumio said in his opening keynote speech to the IISS Shangri-La Dialogue in June 2022, 'Ukraine today may be East Asia tomorrow', and by this he did not merely mean that one regional tragedy might be repeated elsewhere but rather that Europe and East Asia are now connected as one strategic space.[6]

The second reason is that the stakes in a conflict in East Asia, especially one over Taiwan, are even higher than those in Ukraine. In the current state of global rivalry, the incompatibility between the Chinese and American views of the status of that strategically located island – China sees 'the status quo' as entailing a move towards reunification; America and others see it as the avoidance of coercion – is an inherent source of instability. Such a war would be likely to bring the world's two greatest powers into direct military conflict with one another, would be likely to represent a contest for regional and potentially global leadership, and would therefore stand a high chance of drawing other powers into the fight. This is not a new danger, nor one newly observed: in his 2019 *Adelphi* book *Dangerous Decade: Taiwan's Security and Crisis Management*, for example, Brendan Taylor wrote that 'the prospects for a Taiwan conflict are real and intensifying' and that 'they are not yet being treated with the seriousness nor the urgency that they deserve'.[7]

Russia's invasion of Ukraine has changed that, as have the also-intensifying US–China tensions. However, even that heightened seriousness retains elements of unreality, to which the so-far contained and conventional nature of the Ukraine war has perhaps contributed. Taylor's warning that the next Taiwan crisis could readily 'escalate into catastrophic conflict' is still not driving the discussion as much as it should.[8]

Scholars and think tanks frequently come up with scenarios and war games in which a conflict over Taiwan remains contained and conventional.[9] That is, to be sure, the hope of the potential invader. But the question must be asked: if the Chinese and US militaries ever do go into battle with one another, raining down missiles on each other's bases, shooting down each other's aircraft and sinking each other's ships, as such scenarios assume, why should this war not be expected, as a core planning assumption, to escalate? Why would each side not expect, as soon as one opponent starts to feel that it is losing, that the most destructive weapons of all would come into play? After all, Russia has made regular threats to use nuclear weapons since its invasion of Ukraine in February 2022, and while their potential use against Ukrainian forces has lost credibility over time, these threats have been thought sufficiently serious to deter NATO forces from direct intervention.

Is it not stunningly optimistic to assume, as wargamers and scenario workshoppers often seem to do, that China and the US could kill tens of thousands of each other's troops, and potentially face conventional defeat and outcomes which at that point appear strategically existential, but somehow ignore nuclear weapons? In reality, the nuclear question would be ever present in the minds of both sets of political leaders as well as in public opinion in both countries. Just as the archetypically dark Cold War question concerned what might happen if the choice of trading Bonn or Paris for Boston were to present itself, so the inevitable question surrounding the US–China confrontation can be brutally boiled down to, on one side, whether capturing Taiwan would really be worth putting Beijing at risk, and on the other, whether defending Taipei would really be worth risking Los Angeles.

After all, it was just as possible to come up with scenarios during the Cold War in which American and Soviet troops fought limited conventional wars or even limited nuclear ones. However, the risk that such wars would not remain limited was too high and too potentially devastating for such imagined scenarios to be relied upon, so they were not. The worst-case scenario needed to be the one that dictated diplomacy and strategy.

The danger that is hiding in plain sight today is that this fundamental lesson of the Cold War is being overlooked or at best played down. Diplomacy and strategy, indeed, are in part engaged in a tussle over whether a so-called 'Taiwan contingency' should be thought of as a local issue – an 'internal matter' by the Chinese definition – or as merely an unwelcome, violent disturbance to 'the status quo' in the language of some others, or as a conflict that would be central to the US–China contest for strategic dominance and hence with global implications. There are arguments, to be sure, for all three interpretations. But it would be safest for all of us if the prevailing assumption, the one that drove strategy, were the worst of the three. For the likelihood of escalation, and with it catastrophe, is too high to be discounted.

Admittedly, all sides are pursuing strategies that can to differing degrees be described as ones of deterrence, which represent welcome measures to try to prevent a war from starting, and which can also be understood as trying to discourage adversaries from thinking that such a war could be swift or limited in nature. Such conventional means of deterrence can also be thought of as measures to try to convince all sides that a war could be won only through escalation into a major conflict, although the potentially nuclear nature of such a conflict is rarely mentioned, nor even hinted at. Nonetheless, one lesson of the Cold War is that conventional deterrence must be strong and credible enough to prevent any war starting that might make the nuclear sort become necessary. Strong conventional deterrence also makes war less likely to occur because it allows the defender a more credible range of strategic responses, rather than being faced with either acquiescence in the adversary's encroachments or being forced to threaten nuclear apocalypse.

The US has sought, with considerable success, to build a network of allies and partners in the whole Indo-Pacific region – hence 'integrated deterrence' – a network that is largely labelled as sharing the task of deterrence and reinforcing it. It has also adjusted the posture and capabilities of its own forces in the region so as to try to convince China that the risks and costs of an invasion or blockade are too high to make the attempt worthwhile. Taiwan, too, has been pursuing a deterrence strategy by expanding its defence budget and seeking new military capabilities, attempting to convince the potential invader that it would be able to put up costly and sustained resistance. Japan most notably, but also Australia, the Philippines and European NATO countries including the United Kingdom, are all pursuing deterrence strategies, designed to be integrated with those of the US but also hopefully of value on their own.

Moreover, the desire to discourage Taiwan from declaring independence and the US from supporting such a move can also explain China's increased military incursions into Taiwan's Air Defence Identification Zone (ADIZ) and sea space in recent years, its use of intimidatory military exercises, and even the expansion of its nuclear arsenal. Together with the military build-up China has pursued in recent decades, such measures can be seen as efforts to discourage outside intervention in a conflict over Taiwan by making it clear that the ensuing war would be hard fought and potentially escalatory.

The purpose of this *Adelphi* book is to examine these deterrence strategies in the light of the lessons of the Ukraine war and to identify yardsticks with which to gauge their potential effectiveness and, equally important, sustainability over time.

It will thereby seek to 'join the dots' of these various strategies in order to show the overall picture that is emerging, in terms of strengths but crucially also weaknesses. Conventional deterrence is certainly necessary, but it is not likely to be sufficient because of the powerful interests and political psychology that are involved. We must therefore also look at what needs to be built around and alongside these deterrence strategies to increase their chances of success and avoid catastrophe.

Accordingly, the book will take an unashamedly 'big-picture' approach. The author is not someone steeped in the minutiae of missile balances, military acronyms and abbreviations, cross-strait relations or Chinese strategic documents. If anything, he is a Japan specialist rather than an Indo-Pacific analyst, though in a previous book, *Rivals: How the Power Struggle between China, India and Japan Will Shape Our Next Decade*, he made an earlier attempt at painting the larger regional landscape.[10] All those specialisms are highly valuable, but alongside the technical details, scenario workshops and textual analyses, it is in the bigger picture that many of the key, ultimately determining factors lie: in politics, psychology and grand strategy, above all.

The final, and perhaps biggest picture of all is that while the author does not believe that descriptions of today's great-power rivalry as 'a new Cold War' are either accurate or meaningful, in today's conditions there is a need to learn from and ideally reproduce two of the best and most important features of how the Cold War confrontation came to be managed. One was the value of political and strategic consistency over time, even as political parties and leaders change; the other was the value of a diplomatic process of dialogue and negotiations that focuses on the most critical issues, which are Taiwan, arms control and nuclear weapons, for it is only through such a process that anything like a mutual understanding of what is at stake is likely to arise.

Telling ourselves that convincing the US and China to discuss other issues, such as climate, trade or finance, will somehow build understanding and bridge the gaps between them is not just wishful thinking but also a dangerous evasion of reality. The danger is hiding in plain sight. Forcing each other to talk about the real dangers will be enormously difficult and may well take years to achieve, but failing to do so risks something far worse. As Brendan Taylor wrote in this series five years ago, this is a dangerous decade, but future decades promise to be just as dangerous, if not more so.

CHAPTER ONE

Why Indo-Pacific deterrence matters

The 'Doomsday Clock' that was created by the *Bulletin of the Atomic Scientists* in 1947 gets less attention these days than during the Cold War, although perhaps the 2023 film *Oppenheimer* might have revived interest in how close scientists believe the world might be to nuclear or other annihilation. In early 2020, when the *Bulletin* announced that the clock was now set at 100 seconds to midnight, closer to 'doomsday' than at any time during the Cold War, few seemed to notice.[1]

This may in part be because public concern, along with the atomic scientists' own worries, had by then shifted from the threat of man-made nuclear annihilation to the threat of man-made environmental degradation, notably global heating, and that is a long-term threat about which there is much public debate on the appropriate timing and intensity of policy responses. One hundred seconds feels a far less meaningful measure of climate risks, even existential ones, than of nuclear risks. The global coronavirus pandemic that erupted soon after the *Bulletin*'s announcement confirmed the basis for such concern about natural threats but also diverted attention to the here and now.

In the shadows behind the *Bulletin*'s gloomier outlook also stood, however, another more traditional geopolitical concern, which events soon proved to be well founded. This was that after a period of detente and nuclear de-escalation following the fall of the Soviet Union, arms-control treaties between Russia and the United States were breaking down; nuclear proliferation in the new or would-be nuclear-weapons states of North Korea and Iran had returned to prominence; and an increasingly hostile rivalry was taking hold between the two most wide-spectrum superpowers, China and the US, encompassing diplomacy, technology, economics, global governance and military capabilities of all kinds.

Any hopes that the arrival of a common enemy in the form of the novel coronavirus might temper this rivalry and facilitate a new period of cooperation and communication were quickly dashed. After initial collaboration between scientists in China and the rest of the world in sharing the genome of the new virus, and then in trade of the personal protective equipment and other supplies vital for treatment and containment, the great-power rivals essentially responded to the pandemic separately, trading barbs about the virus's Chinese origins and competing over the development and international supply of vaccines and treatments. Russia, too, produced its own vaccine and resisted collaboration with the West. And even before many countries had declared the pandemic to be over, military confrontation between Russia and its neighbours resumed.

To those who noticed, it should then have been unsurprising that in January 2023 the *Bulletin* raised its alarm level even higher, by moving the figurative hands of the Doomsday Clock again, to 90 seconds to midnight and then leaving them there in January 2024.[2] If the public imagination had indeed shifted towards climate as presenting the greatest existential threat, Russian President Vladimir Putin had done his best to seize back that territory of the imagination alongside his attempted seizure in February 2022 of the entire territory of Ukraine by overtly threatening nuclear-weapons use to try to deter the West from intervening.

Certainly, the risk of Russia breaking the eight-decades-long taboo by using a nuclear weapon remains terrifying, as does the consequent need for American and other NATO leaders to make plans for how they would respond if that were to happen. Yet this, alas, is not even the biggest current reason to fear nuclear apocalypse.

The biggest reason for concern lies in the rivalry between the US and the rising power of China, and the fact that the perceived stakes in that truly global rivalry are becoming so high. Those stakes make a direct conflict between China and the US look likelier than one between Russia and the US, whether by accident or design. And they mean that, if such a conflict were to occur, there would be a real prospect that both the threat and the use of nuclear weapons could come to make strategic sense to either side, and then to both. Such a conflict, even if it began over the seemingly local issue of Taiwan, could quickly come to represent a tussle not just for regional but also for global leadership, one that neither side would feel it could afford to lose.

During 2021 and 2022, US President Joe Biden made his perception of this difference in stakes explicit. He deliberately and carefully ruled out the physical participation in the Ukraine war of US or NATO forces, saying that 'he did not intend to start World War Three' by fighting Russia directly.[3] But in October 2021 and then again in May 2022, this US commander-in-chief made a clear pledge that if China were to attempt to use force to take over Taiwan, the US military would intervene directly to prevent it.[4] He repeated this pledge twice more during 2022.

Biden's White House staff and the State Department each time followed up with a 'clarification' that his statement did not imply any change to America's long-standing agreements with China, which date back to 1972, about Taiwan and the so-called 'One China' policy.[5] In all those agreements, the US has made clear its opposition to the use of force to bring about a resolution of the status of Taiwan but has deliberately avoided stating any view over the rightful status of the islands.

What Biden's pledges did do, however, was to overturn a previous convention, not contained in those US–China agreements, of 'strategic ambiguity', maintained so as not to be seen to encourage Taiwanese independence by promising to protect the island in all and any circumstances.[6] Biden's decision to emphasise his policy of strategic clarity suggests that in the wake of Russia's invasion of Ukraine and the Russo-Chinese Joint Statement, he felt that the risk of a Chinese invasion of Taiwan was sufficiently high that he needed to deter it by stating his willingness to engage directly in such a conflict.[7]

Why the stakes in Taiwan are so high

If that willingness is genuine and is maintained by subsequent US presidents, then it means more than just that the US would be willing to sail a couple of aircraft carriers to the Taiwan Strait to act as a warning to China, as then-president Bill Clinton did in 1996 when there was a previous crisis over Taiwan. It means that the country with the world's most powerful military force would be willing to fight a war with the country that has the world's second-most powerful military force, one that has the advantage of greater proximity to and concentration on Taiwan. It would also therefore have to mean that America would be willing to take the risk that such a conflict could involve the first use of nuclear weapons since atomic bombs were dropped on Hiroshima and Nagasaki in 1945, for such a risk arises inevitably in a fight between fellow nuclear powers. By the same token, if China were to take the military actions that prompted an American military intervention, it would mean that it too had decided it was willing to fight a war against the US and to take the risk of the war escalating into a much larger and even nuclear one.

This may well involve a series of bluffs: China could rationally emulate Putin by using a nuclear threat to try to persuade America to stand aside and allow it to treat Taiwan as an internal matter, thus keeping the war local and conventional; America could call China's bluff by positioning some of its forces so as to make it clear that if China proceeds with an invasion it will have no choice but to fight the US military and thus to dare it to take both that risk and the risk of nuclear escalation in a confrontation with a far stronger nuclear power. Such bluffs would be the military equivalent of a car drivers' (or game theorists') 'game of chicken', in which each player might bet that the other will in fact back down. And, as in the game of driving at each other at high speed, they could be proven wrong, with catastrophic consequences.

This Indo-Pacific game of chicken is more complicated than that of the car drivers, for the decision-making and bluff-calling involve three sets of political leaders, not two: those in Beijing, Washington DC and Taipei. Russia's Ukraine invasion in 2022 made anything seem possible. Nonetheless, although tensions between Beijing, Taipei and Washington are currently high, the prospect of a major war does not look imminent, which may be why Biden did not feel it necessary to repeat his deterrent message in 2023. Even so, the prospect and the potential consequences look so serious and severe as to merit correspondingly careful preparations from all sides.

In talks during the Nixon–Kissinger opening of US–China dialogue in 1971–72 and beyond, leaders of the People's Republic of China (PRC) often expressed pessimism about the likelihood that reunification with Taiwan could be peaceful.

In 1979, during an official visit to the US, China's then-leader Deng Xiaoping even defined circumstances in which force would be necessary: while it would be alright for Taiwan to refuse talks with the PRC for one or two years, he said, if the refusal persisted for a long time, for example ten years, then it would necessarily lead to settlement by use of force.[8]

There have now in fact been no high-level talks between the PRC and Taiwan's government since 2016, although this reflects a refusal on the side of the PRC rather than Taiwan. The election as Taiwan's president that year of Tsai Ing-wen, whom China considers to be a separatist, led the PRC to put a freeze on dialogue.[9]

Throughout her two terms of office (2016–24) president Tsai offered to work with the Beijing authorities to preserve peace and stability 'provided there is rationality, equality and mutual respect'.[10] But those words were carefully chosen and have been used equally carefully by her successor and former vice-president, Lai Ching-te, following his election as president on 13 January 2024. They both know that 'equality' is exactly the basis on which the PRC is not willing to talk, for to do so would violate a cherished principle that Taiwan is a 'renegade province' of China, not an equivalent state.

That lack of talks, and the related severing since 2016 of the military hotline that previously connected the two sides of the Taiwan Strait, has coincided with a steady increase in Chinese military pressure on the island through daily flights of a variety of military aircraft into Taiwan's Air Defence Identification Zone (ADIZ), and through highly demonstrative military exercises.[11] Previous norms concerning the median demarcation line in the Taiwan Strait between China and Taiwan are now being ignored, and China is also conducting naval operations just outside Taiwan's territorial waters.[12]

As a result, a macabre kind of parlour game has got under way in Washington, Beijing, Taipei and many capital cities in the Indo-Pacific of making predictions or evaluations of the likelihood of a Chinese attack on Taiwan or of Taiwan's coercion through some sort of Chinese blockade. That game had already been spiced up by comments in 2021 to the Senate Armed Services Committee in Washington by the then-commander of the US Indo-Pacific Command, Admiral Philip Davidson, that in his view, an invasion could come 'in the next six years'.[13]

Nevertheless, an unscientific summary of the current consensus of these evaluations, as garnered during research interviews for this book, would be that the closer one gets to Taiwan itself, the lower is the assigned likelihood of an imminent attack, despite all those intimidating Chinese military manoeuvres. This is no doubt partly a result of living with the possibility of a conflict for so long, which may bring with it a psychology of denial, but seems also to be because closeness brings an increased appreciation of how difficult an attempted invasion would be, whether in the commonly imagined forms of an amphibious landing or of an attempted lightning 'decapitation' of Taiwan's government by means of an airborne assault on Taipei.

Proximity does, however, bring an opposing impression too: the closer one gets to Taiwan, the greater is the appreciation of the high stakes that are involved. Perhaps proximity should now be defined more widely than just as Taiwan itself, for appreciation of those high stakes feels as if it is just as high in Tokyo as in Taipei.

There are three reasons why the stakes over Taiwan now look higher than ever before:

1. History and status

As notes and transcripts of discussions between Henry Kissinger, Richard Nixon, Zhou Enlai, Mao Zedong and others show, the role of Taiwan as the final vestige of two twentieth-century wars – the Chinese Civil War (1927–36; 1945–49) between the Communists and Nationalists, and the Sino-Japanese wars of 1894–95 and 1937–45 – has always been prominent and has long been an issue on which PRC leaders would brook no compromise.[14]

While Taiwan was governed by the man and the army that the Communists had defeated in 1949, Chiang Kai-shek of the Kuomintang party, the PRC's aim of completing its victory was particularly evident, but he died in 1975 and his son Chiang Ching-kuo died in 1988, having ended martial law the previous year. Taiwan's eventual transformation into a democracy (1991–96) might have been hoped to lessen that imperative by finally ending the delusion that the island was home to a rival government in exile, but it has not. Democracy and generational change have brought a burgeoning Taiwanese identity as an autonomous nation. Meanwhile, now that Chinese President Xi Jinping has defined his goal as 'the great rejuvenation of the Chinese nation', the desire to bring Taiwan back under Chinese rule has become a key symbol of that rejuvenation.[15]

The history of Chinese rule is rather different from the version given by official PRC propaganda, under which Taiwan has supposedly 'been an inalienable part of China since ancient times'.[16] A more neutral historical account would be that in what most would deem as 'ancient times', this was an independent island with an indigenous population, which received some settlers from the mainland, was named 'Ilha Formosa' or 'beautiful island' by Portuguese travellers in the sixteenth century, and then had small colonies established by the Dutch and the Spanish in the early seventeenth century. The Dutch East India Company brought in more Chinese settlers, chiefly as labourers. A Chinese pirate, Zheng Chenggong (also known as Koxinga), defeated the Dutch in 1662 and used the island as his personal fief and base.[17]

Taiwan was annexed by the Qing Dynasty of China only in 1683, following which large numbers of mainland settlers arrived and displaced the indigenous population. It became designated as a province only in 1887. Moreover, if the territory of China as defined by the areas ruled by the Manchu-led Qing Dynasty is to be used to demarcate 'the motherland', then the country now called the Republic of Mongolia should also form part of China's claims, which it does not.[18]

Thus, Taiwan and its associated islands were administered by China only for two centuries up to China's 1895 defeat in the First Sino-Japanese War, when Taiwan was ceded to Japan under the Treaty of Shimonoseki. Formally speaking, following Japan's defeat in 1945, it then became part of Nationalist China until 1949, when the Nationalist Kuomintang was itself defeated and set up its own government there, suppressing local opposition brutally. In sum, Taiwan spent a lot less time under rule by Imperial China (two centuries) than, for example, Ireland did under English rule (eight centuries), and no one today would dare suggest that the proudly independent Irish should really belong to Britain as they had 'been an inalienable part of England since ancient times'.

The psychological importance Taiwan holds for the PRC and for its narrative is not the result of studying archives and old maps. It is a matter of the perceived imperative of finally and victoriously concluding more recent history – those wars of the twentieth century – and above all maintaining or building China's reputation and status in the world, and in the eyes of the Chinese public. The consequence is that no PRC leader could afford to give up on the goal of reunification with Taiwan, but also that no PRC leader would likely be able to survive a failed attempt to enforce such a reunification.

2. Regional strategy and maritime control

For decades, the Taiwan issue was commonly presented as being chiefly about history and reputation. Recently, however, the intensification of great-power rivalry has transferred attention towards geography. Taiwan's location gives it potential strategic control over the South China Sea, to Taiwan's southwest, and the East China Sea, to its north. From Taiwan leads what is known as the 'first island chain', running south through the Philippines and north up Japan's long string of islands, known as the Nansei or Ryukyu, past Okinawa to Kyushu, Japan's southernmost main island (see Map 2).

There is nothing new about this. But while China and its neighbours were poor and weak, strategic issues such as maritime control of the seas around the country's 18,000-kilometre coastline may not have felt imminent or practical. Moreover, to focus on history provided the PRC with a more favourable narrative, especially vis-à-vis its neighbours, than to talk about maritime control over seas in the midst of which those neighbours also reside.

This has changed. An influential book, *Red Star Over the Pacific*, first published in 2010 and now in its third edition, by two professors from the US Naval War College on how American and Chinese maritime strategies in Asia are competing, cites Zhu Tingchang, an analyst from the School of International Relations in the People's Liberation Army's (PLA) National Defense University in Nanjing, as writing that:

> For China to develop in the Pacific, it must charge out of the first island chain. And the key to charging out of the first island chain is Taiwan. Taiwan is China's front gate to the Pacific. If the Taiwan question is not resolved, then it is akin to a lock around the neck of a great dragon.[19]

Map 2: **East Asia and the two island chains**

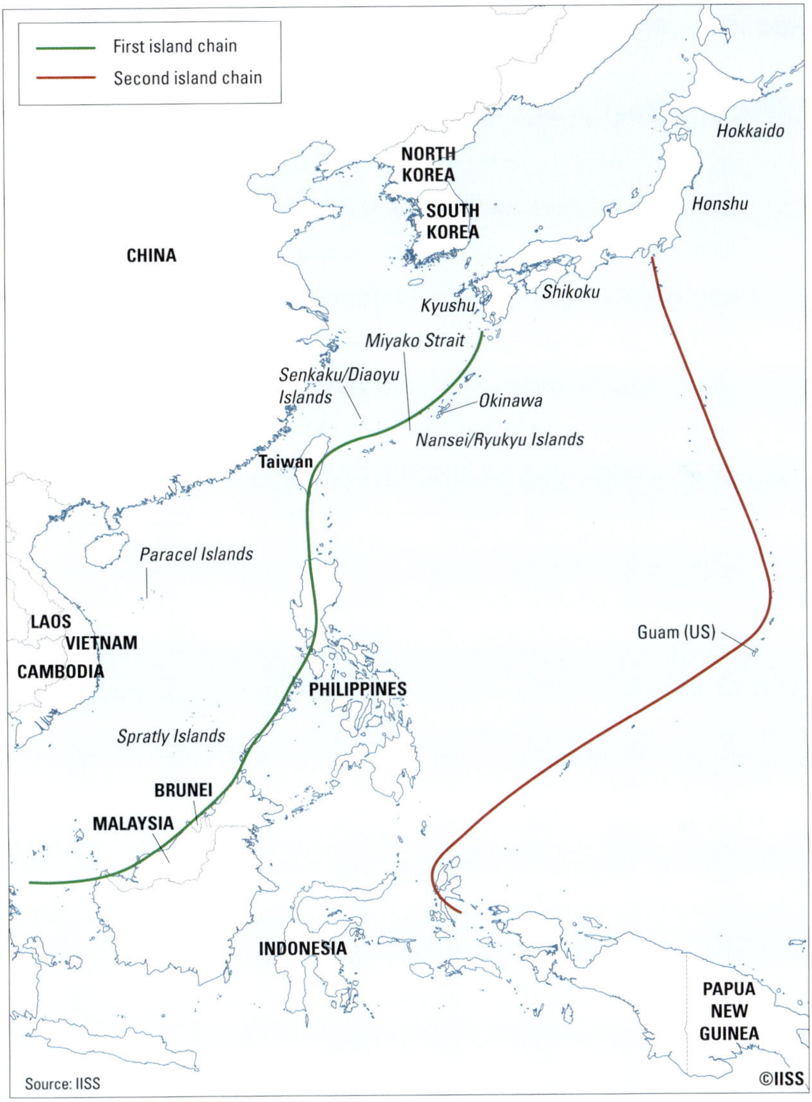

— First island chain
— Second island chain

The American book's authors, Toshi Yoshihara and James Holmes, place that quotation in the context of wider Chinese analysis, notably in the PLA's doctrinal *Science of Military Strategy*, of the key role being played by Taiwan in what is held to be America's containment strategy for China and of Taiwan's role as an 'essential strategic space for China's rejuvenation'.[20]

They further quote two authors from that work, Shi Chunlin and Li Xiuying, as arguing that:

> Taiwan's unification with the Chinese mainland would snap the central waist of the first island chain that the United States and its allies have so carefully constructed. It would also substantially reduce the strategic value of the [Japanese] Ryukyu Islands, which are strategically interdependent with Taiwan. This would mean that the first island chain would completely collapse as an American and allied instrument for blockading China. The United States would have no choice but to retreat to the second island chain.[21]

The argument, in essence, is that the loss of Taiwan would lead to the unravelling of the US alliance system in Asia, as Chinese pressure would then be brought to bear directly on the Philippines, Japan and South Korea. It is not entirely clear why, as Shi and Li argue, US forces would then have to be withdrawn entirely from those countries and moved to Guam (the 'second island chain'), but we can imagine that in circumstances that had led to a non-peaceful Chinese takeover of Taiwan – a major war – a forward US deployment in those countries might no longer be feasible. The real way to push America out of the Western Pacific, on this argument, is to capture Taiwan and to win the associated war.

Some would argue that China is already taking control over that maritime area, with or without Taiwan. China's construction of military bases on reefs and shoals in disputed areas of the South China Sea over the past decade – it now has 20 outposts in the Paracel Islands and seven in the Spratlys – have been viewed as moves towards making control over that sea possible, as has direct Chinese harassment of areas claimed by the Philippines and others.[22] The same is said of Chinese maritime harassment of the Japanese Senkaku islands (known in China as the Diaoyu Dao) in the East China Sea.

This ambition, or at least perspective, is also already displayed in China's expansive territorial claims over the entire area, which were restated by its new official 'standard map' in September 2023, a map that clashed with the claims of at least six countries (see Map 3).[23] There was nothing terribly new in this map or its claims, but the inclusion not only of the notorious 'nine-dash line', a huge tongue-shaped area denoting claimed control of the entire South China Sea, but also of a tenth dash to the east of Taiwan, served to reiterate the Chinese view that this maritime area is China's own strategic zone. That dashed line was in fact first put forward by Chiang Kai-shek's Kuomintang government in 1948 in the form of 11 dashes, two of which were removed by Chairman Mao in 1952.

When Japan's then-prime minister, Abe Shinzo, advocated in 2012 and formalised in 2016 the idea that maintaining a 'Free and Open Indo-Pacific' (FOIP) should be a core objective not just for the West but also for all littoral nations of those oceans, what he particularly hoped to rally support behind was the goal of preventing any single nation from controlling either the South China or East China seas, for those are the only truly 'closeable' parts of the Indo-Pacific.[24] The only nation deemed likely to threaten a FOIP is China. The one nation that China sees as capable of obstructing that strategic control is the US.

The potential consequences of Chinese control over the Western Pacific for the countries of that region – which include Japan, South Korea and all the members of the Association of Southeast Asian Nations (ASEAN) – would be momentous. The sea lanes passing through into the two China seas and thus the Western Pacific are the world's busiest. If one country were to

Map 3: **China's territorial claims**

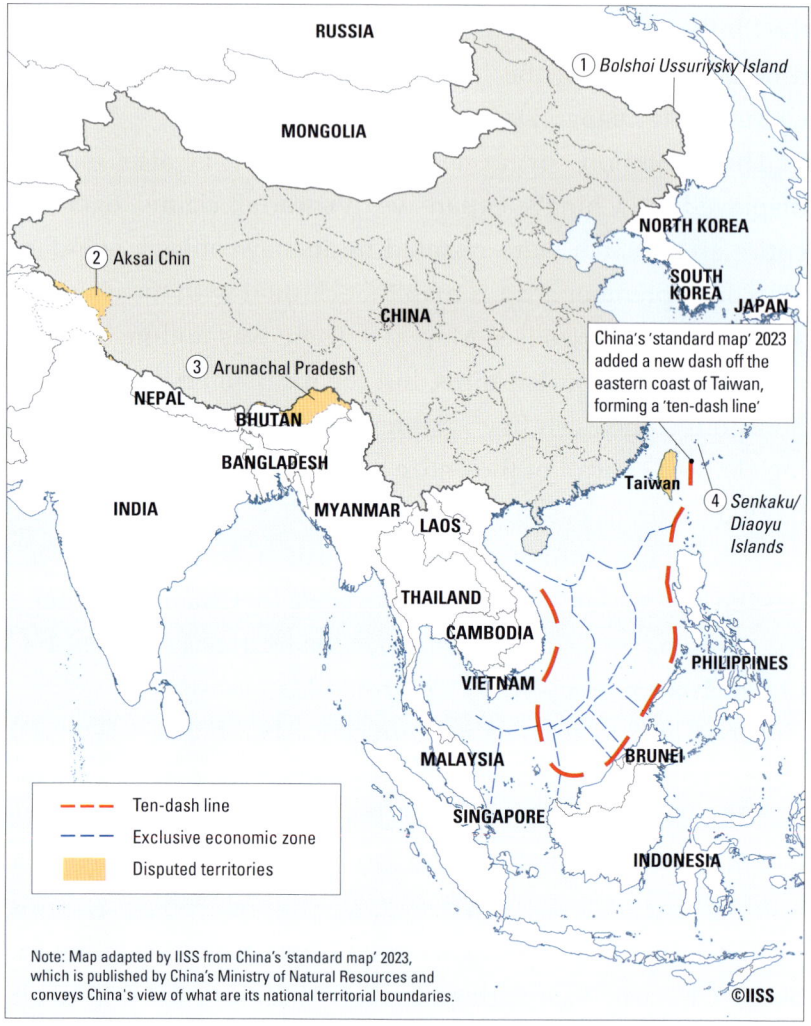

China's 'standard map' 2023 added a new dash off the eastern coast of Taiwan, forming a 'ten-dash line'

- - - Ten-dash line
- - - Exclusive economic zone
▨ Disputed territories

Note: Map adapted by IISS from China's 'standard map' 2023, which is published by China's Ministry of Natural Resources and conveys China's view of what are its national territorial boundaries.

©IISS

Location	Notes
① Bolshoi Ussuriysky Island	Divided between Russia and China under 2004 agreement, but still all claimed by China
② Aksai Chin	Administered by China; claimed by India
③ Arunachal Pradesh	Administered by India; claimed by China
④ Senkaku/Diaoyu Islands	Administered by Japan; claimed by China

Sources: IISS; China's Ministry of Natural Resources; JAPAN Forward

gain control over the flow of commerce and military supplies, it would gain enormous leverage over the political economy of every nation in that region.

3. Global significance

At a time of peace, of globally accepted rules of conduct and open trade, control over such a maritime area would not be a live issue. But we are now in a time of contestation of those rules, of the institutions of collective governance that oversee them, and of the distribution of power in the world.

The world has seen great-power rivalry many times before: historically it is the norm.[25] Yet it was precisely to try to manage great-power rivalry that new rules and institutions were established after 1945, with the United Nations Charter as the founding document, one that has been built on with new institutions and new rules in the decades since, regionally and globally. That founding document was signed by the Soviet Union and by then-Nationalist China. While any challenge to global rules and the process by which they are made can be simply pursued in politics and diplomacy, the fact that the Russo-Chinese Joint Statement was followed just three weeks later by Russia's invasion of Ukraine confirms that the challenge can easily take military form too.[26]

Taiwan may look like a local issue, but its strategic location combined with this broader rivalry between the great powers gives it global significance. During the Cold War between the West and the Soviet Union, there were numerous cases in which seemingly local issues took on global importance – the Korean War in 1950–53, above all Cuba in 1962, Vietnam, and a host of proxy wars in Africa and Latin America – thanks to the framing reality of great-power rivalry. In hindsight the remarkable fact is that none of them produced a direct military confrontation between the two nuclear superpowers, but several times, most notably with Cuba, it was a close-run thing.

Not surprisingly, security literature, both scholarly and popular, has come to reflect the danger that out of this great-power contest and the Taiwan flashpoint could easily come a major conflict. Just as during the Cold War, the high and genuinely global stakes between the great powers mean that the burden of proof on whether such a conflict would turn nuclear must lie on those who assume it would not. For when great powers that possess the most devastating weapons come to fight each other with global leadership at stake, it is surely implausible that the use of those weapons would not be seriously contemplated. The consequences of their use would be so catastrophic that to make a limited war the base scenario is a kind of wilful blindness.

One of the most notable recent warnings was *The Avoidable War: The Dangers of a Catastrophic Conflict between the US and Xi Jinping's China*, a powerful 2022 contribution written by former Australian prime minister Kevin Rudd during his time leading the Asia Society in New York.[27] With this book Rudd, who is a Mandarin-speaking former diplomat, was in effect arguing that as the rising potential for war merits recommendations on how it can be avoided, in the absence of such actions a war must be considered probable. He advocates the establishment of what he terms 'managed strategic competition', which is in line with the conclusion of this *Adelphi* book, except that while rightly warning of catastrophe he dismisses the idea of such a conflict turning nuclear rather unconvincingly.[28] Rudd re-entered diplomacy as Australia's ambassador to the US in March 2023.[29]

Five years earlier, Graham Allison, a seasoned and sober political scientist at the Harvard Kennedy School of Government, had published a now widely cited historical study of confrontations between established and rising powers, asking *Can America and China Escape Thucydides's Trap?*[30] Allison's scholarly answer was that statistically such wars between incumbent and rising powers – famously identified by the Greek historian Thucydides in the fears and rivalry in ancient Greece between

Athens and Sparta – have happened more often than not, with the implication that, as Rudd later also argued, hard work would be required if the statistical record was to be beaten.

The long duration of China's rise, with the transformative effect it has had on the world economy and global politics, made it logical to examine this danger in the Thucydidean framework. Chinese political speeches and propaganda have reinforced this through the repeated assertion that the US and the West are in decline while China is amid its 'great rejuvenation'.

Recently, however, another potential framework has emerged. It is that with China's population now declining and its structure ageing, the era of seemingly effortless Chinese economic strength may be over.[31] If that proves to be so, although China would remain powerful, its potential rise would be capped by the combination of that demographic structure and the domestic political and economic rigidities that have developed over the past decade or so.

In that case, although China's relative economic power might decline, its leaders' incentive to try to gain strategic control over Taiwan and the Western Pacific might rise. Time might no longer seem as if it is on China's side. The desire to compensate for economic disappointment by making strategic gains could increase, whether for purely nationalistic reasons or for more mercenary ones. Moreover, a moment when a China conscious of its own future weakness perceives a corresponding period of weakness on the American side could be the most dangerous of all.

The conflict to be deterred

The task is clear: to prevent a conflict over Taiwan from ever becoming a serious prospect. An overarching reason to prevent that conflict from ever happening is the possibility, which for planning purposes should be thought of as a likelihood, that a

US–China war would turn nuclear. That is both why conventional deterrence is so important – the barriers against this potential war need to be high – and why on its own it cannot be considered sufficient.

As Europe has just seen a broad contest turning into a hot war, with a rather fuzzily conceived set of deterrence, diplomacy and communications strategies failing to prevent Russia's invasion of Ukraine, the next chapter will explore what lessons can be learned from that deterrence failure for the task in the Indo-Pacific.

CHAPTER TWO

Deterrence lessons from Ukraine

The immediate background to all thinking about deterrence in the Indo-Pacific must be the experience of Ukraine. This is because of China's diplomatic complicity in Russia's actions through the February 2022 Joint Statement, and because such fresh experience is likely to weigh heavily on the thinking of political or military policymakers all over the world, and on public attitudes in all the countries concerned.

With the war still under way, it is not possible to draw firm conclusions. But at the time of writing, there look to be eight main lessons from Ukraine that are relevant to those aspects of deterrence in the Indo-Pacific.

Eight lessons from Ukraine

1. Economic or financial sanctions may punish, but the threat of them does not deter

In theory, the threat of punishment is considered a valid tool of deterrence. However, experience of the 2014 sanctions imposed on Russia following the annexation of Crimea and the covert seizure of the Donbas region, and then of the far more stringent sanctions imposed on Russia by a larger coalition of countries following the February 2022 full invasion, shows that fear of such economic punishment did not deter President Vladimir Putin from doing what he wanted to do.[1] And having seen the impact of such punishment on Russia, it would be extremely unlikely that fear of sanctions would affect Chinese thinking about an invasion or blockade of Taiwan.

Despite their unprecedented severity and breadth, the 2022 sanctions have failed to have an impact on the Russian economy or public finances sufficient to have a major near-term influence over Russia's political or military calculations. Russian exports of fossil fuels and other commodities have still found plenty of willing buyers. Willing suppliers continue to exist for many goods, including some of military use, enabling the economy to continue to function, public welfare to be maintained and public finances to be sustained. The sanctions and the pressure on Russian production and stockpiles from the war led Putin to court North Korea's Kim Jong-un as an arms supplier, in a way he would not have considered necessary or appropriate before 2022, but this just confirms that despite sanctions, a country of Russia's scale, resources and relationships does have options.[2]

Eventually, shortages of components, especially sophisticated semiconductors, and of ammunition may play a bigger part in the war, but there is no evidence that any Chinese study of the Russian experience under sanctions would be likely to show a significant deterrent effect or threat. The broad lesson for China is that a large, wealthy economy still with a wide range of trading partners can adapt itself to withstand even drastic economic or financial sanctions. China, the world's second-largest economy and one for which external trade holds a declining importance, is likely to judge itself even more able to withstand sanctions than Russia has been. It has some vulnerabilities in terms of imports of energy, but through stockpiles and domestic substitution has some scope to deal with these. In the event of a major war with the United States, such import dependencies could become an important factor, but more because of the associated massive disruption of trade – which would be far greater than is the case for Russia's war in Ukraine – rather than sanctions.

2. Economic impacts play little short-term role when the political stakes are high

A related lesson from Ukraine is that, regardless of sanctions and their effectiveness, a great power run by a dictatorial regime can disregard the economic consequences of its military actions, both for itself and for other countries, at least in the short term. In the end, the decision will depend on how important the action is to the invader. In Russia's case, Putin has shown that his country can afford to turn itself into a war economy, with the greatly increased spending on arms and defence-equipment production helping to support incomes and employment. Understanding the motivation of the counterpart is vital for any deterrence strategy as it is otherwise impossible to make useful cost–benefit calculations: in the case of Putin, it is clear with hindsight that his motivations were misjudged, at least by the West.

The likely cost of a war over Taiwan would be huge – just as the cost of the twentieth century's two world wars was huge – but is also inherently unpredictable because it would be dependent on the level of escalation and the duration of any war.[3] In any case, when a state or a dictator is seeking outcomes considered to be of historical, civilisational or strategic importance – or all three – economic impacts become secondary. The principal relevance of economics lies in whether the progenitor of a war with every prospect of escalating and enduring believes that their country's capacity for military production and for maintaining military forces will exceed that of their opponents.

3. Psychology plays a crucial role, especially in a regime in which power is concentrated in the hands of a few

When it became evident in late 2021 that Russian forces were massing on the borders of Ukraine, it still seemed reasonable to doubt whether Putin would order an invasion despite plenty of warnings from the US that this was his plan. The invasion force looked too small, the risks too high, the consequences of a war too unpredictable. Yet he still went ahead – and as we now know, any idea he may have had about achieving a rapid and fairly easy victory proved to be tragically wrong. Such widespread scepticism about whether the massing of forces could be anything more than a bluff occurred even though he had previously given abundant evidence of his thinking about what he saw as the rightful relationship between Russia and Ukraine.[4]

The first part of this lesson is that it pays to take what dictators write and say seriously, for they may actually mean it. The second part is arguably more important: it is that analysis of the rationality of a decision needs to be set in the context of the psychology of the person or group making that decision. When that person is a dictator, surrounded by a small group of loyalists, a special issue arises: the impact of power, especially near-absolute power, on the brain itself. Professor Ian Robertson, professor of psychology at Trinity College Dublin, wrote presciently in 2014 in *Psychology Today* of 'The Danger that Lurks Inside Vladimir Putin's Brain':

> There can be little doubt that his brain has been neurologically and physically changed so much that he firmly and genuinely believes that without him, Russia is doomed. Absolute power for long periods

makes you blind to risk, highly egocentric, narcissistic and utterly devoid of self-awareness.[5]

The evidence of Putin's invasion in 2022 and of his behaviour since lends credence to this diagnosis as well as indicating a need for caution in making judgements about the likely impact of deterrent threats on the decision-making of such powerful individuals.[6] Like Putin, President Xi Jinping has cast aside restraints on the power of his office, notably the previous two-term limit for Chinese presidents. It is not yet clear that he is as isolated and surrounded by sycophants as Putin, but he is known to have purged opponents and installed loyalists.[7] The lesson of the Ukraine invasion must be to cast doubt on conventional assignments of rationality and in particular of checks and balances on such a dictatorial figure's decision-making.

For such an individual power-holder, it could even come to seem more risky or fateful not to take action than to take it, even when advised that the chances of success are poor. Albeit in a different context, that is what happened when Japan chose to attack the US Navy at Pearl Harbor in 1941. Japanese naval chief Admiral Yamamoto Isoroku had opposed the attack and then had to carry it out, following which he reportedly wrote in his diary that 'I fear all we have done is to awaken a sleeping giant and fill him with a terrible resolve'.[8]

4. The timing and speed of Western responses have been key variables

As a result of Russia's military successes in 2014, Western supporters provided considerable amounts of training for Ukrainian military forces as well as extensive intelligence assistance and contributions to national cyber resilience. That support, of which Russia will have been aware, did not deter the invasion, for Putin appears to have expected Russia's forces to be able to defeat Ukraine in just a few days or at most weeks. Since the invasion, Western governments have likely surprised both Russia and China with the extent and sustainability of their military and economic support for Ukraine, but not by the speed of their decision-making or delivery of military supplies.

With the war still under way, we cannot yet know for how long Western support for Ukraine will be maintained. But we can also assume that Chinese planners will have noted that while Western support for Ukraine has surprised on the upside, the process by which it has arrived has been slow and cumbersome, even though the existence of land borders with supportive states such as Poland makes it easier in principle than would be the case for Taiwan. The wider the coalition from which support is derived, the more cumbersome that decision-making process becomes. The task for the US of marshalling that support, as de facto leader of the Ukraine-supporting coalition, has been time-consuming and difficult – although America's own decisions have also been complicated by President Joe Biden's calculations about risk and more recently by the grip on the Republican Party held by his predecessor and again electoral opponent in 2024, Donald Trump.

This gives the initiator of a conflict a considerable advantage, even if – thanks to US intelligence capabilities – their preparations may be noticed well in advance, just as Russia's were, and given the experience of Ukraine such warnings might be trusted next time. Based on the Ukraine example, a Chinese planner may reasonably judge that by the time broader Western support for Taiwan arrived in sufficient quantity to make a difference, the invasion could already be won (or lost). The deterrent effect of perceptions of the likelihood and extent of that support would therefore depend critically on calculations of the potential duration of any action or conflict. This will change only if there are credible grounds for believing that external support and/or direct military intervention would arrive quickly enough to make a material difference.

5. Ukrainian political and public resilience has been a prerequisite for garnering and maintaining outside support

The primary arguments made by Western governments in condemning Russia's invasion of Ukraine and justifying their support for Ukraine and Ukrainians have been legal, moral and geographical: that changing the borders of another sovereign country by force violates the UN Charter and thus international law; that depriving a sovereign, independent people of their freedom without due cause is simply wrong; and that a Russian conquest of Ukraine puts other neighbours at risk, including Poland, the Baltic states and Moldova. Yet the timing, extent and duration of Western support have also been highly dependent on a quite different principle: whether Ukraine appears deserving or undeserving. This has some overlap with the moral argument, but in practice the decisive issue has been whether Ukrainians are willing to fight for their own freedom, and how well their fight has been going.

President Volodymyr Zelenskyy's decision to refuse the offer of evacuation on 24–25 February 2022, saying he wanted 'ammunition not a ride', was central to this, a demonstration of determination to stay and fight that was repeated and displayed globally through a highly effective communications strategy.[9] But so too has been evidence, shared widely through the media, of the Ukrainian public's eagerness to fight and to resist.

6. Escalation, especially through nuclear threats, has played a big role

The Russian nuclear threats made during 2022 were a limited form of escalation dominance, a strategy much theorised about during the Cold War: the credible use of warnings of more powerful retaliation than an adversary can or is willing to deploy to shape that adversary's behaviour. Putin's threats of going nuclear can be said to have succeeded by deterring Western governments from immediately supplying Ukraine with their most advanced weaponry – or at least by slowing down their decisions to supply such weaponry – and certainly by ruling out any possibility that NATO forces would join the war directly, for example to establish and police so-called 'no-fly zones'. The threat gained time for the Russians, albeit arguably at the eventual cost of credibility.

Ukraine confirms that the credible threat of escalation to a wider and more cataclysmic war can have a powerful deterrent effect. But unlike in the case of Ukraine, where the US made no commitment to defend the country directly, for Taiwan the threat – and the deterrent effect – could go in either direction, depending on the perceived willingness to deploy it.

7. The absence of committed outside forces acts as an encouragement

Russia and its supporters have been quick to use the supply of NATO weaponry to Ukraine as an excuse to label the conflict as a proxy war between NATO and Russia. This follows on from the argument that it was the enlargement of NATO to include the formerly Russian-controlled countries of Central and Eastern Europe, along with brief talk in 2008 of a possible future path into NATO for Ukraine, that provoked Russia into invading, supposedly to protect its own security interests.

Yet this simply underlines the gap between claims about the legitimacy of military action and the reality of the conflict itself. The reality learned from the actual war has been that the unwillingness of NATO countries to get directly involved in fighting Russia has created the space for Putin to act and to maintain Russia's control over large parts of Ukraine's territory.

Consequently, a key question surrounding a Taiwan invasion or blockade concerns the perceived likelihood that American or other countries' forces would swiftly and directly become involved, or whether they would – as in Ukraine – focus on supplying the Taiwanese to support their resistance.

8. Narratives of cause and justification can be powerful

Russia has provoked much ridicule for its official claim that its invasion of Ukraine is merely a 'special military operation' rather than a war, ridicule that has even spread to inside Russia. Despite that, a further deterrence-related lesson from Ukraine is that efforts to shape the narrative through direct campaigning and propaganda, and through disinformation, can affect both attitudes to the conflict around the world and willingness to act in support of one side or the other. This narrative has taken many forms, including the arguments about the provocative and threatening effect of NATO enlargement, Putin's own arguments about Ukrainian history and culture, claims of Western double standards, and attempts to portray Ukrainians not as victims but as culpable aggressors in various ways.

Such Russian efforts have not been entirely successful, and whatever initial success might have been achieved through claims that Ukrainian leaders were 'fascists' or 'Nazis' has faded over time, although more outside Russia than inside. Nonetheless, the broader lesson is that the politics and psychology of participation in a conflict are susceptible to such narratives.

Specific implications for China

This chapter has already alluded to some of the lessons from Ukraine for Chinese military planners or political leaders who might be contemplating military action against Taiwan. The most important ones, however, look to begin with the basic fact that a successful invasion of a neighbouring country is hard and risky, even for a superpower.[10]

As an island, Taiwan would be easier to isolate from allies' supplies than Ukraine, but also harder to conquer by conventional means: an amphibious landing would need to be the largest such effort since the Allied landings on D-Day in 1944, and would bear considerable risks of being slowed or obstructed, especially by undersea warfare. This makes escalation to limit such obstruction – through airborne attacks on Taiwanese bases and allied bases in other countries, and even through nuclear threats – look more necessary, but that too raises the potential costs and risks of action.

Key failures in Russia's February 2022 invasion were its inability to capture or kill Ukraine's civilian and military leadership, along with a failure to anticipate the will of Ukrainian society to resist. Absent a credible strategy to 'decapitate' Taiwan's leadership in the opening period of a campaign, China's chances of success would similarly be reduced, and the risks of escalation increased. Time therefore plays a critical role in the dynamics of internal resistance in a target country and of external support for the target. If adversaries can convince China that it cannot succeed at speed, this could have a strong deterrent effect. To the contrary, if Chinese planners come to believe that rapid success is achievable, this could encourage them to downplay or disregard the potential costs and risks of a long-drawn-out conflict.

Command of the narrative can play a significant role in shaping both internal resistance and external support. In the case of Taiwan, China's framing narrative – that Taiwan is a 'renegade province', any dispute with which is an 'internal matter' for 'the Chinese people' to decide, with the Taiwanese defined as being part of the Chinese people – is already strongly established and will have an important impact on external views of any conflict. However, the strength of this narrative has diminished considerably inside Taiwan in recent years. Meanwhile, externally, a rival narrative, of Taiwan as a flourishing liberal democracy of 23.4 million people, has gained a strong foothold, especially in the West, but also in some parts of East and Southeast Asia.[11] For littoral countries of the South China and East China seas, a further narrative of China as an expansionist bully seeking to extend its maritime control over the whole area and to seize territory reinforces this sympathy for Taiwan, whose own 'one China'-based claims over those seas and territories have lost credibility even if officially they remain in place.

Specific implications for Taiwan

Taiwan has been preparing for a potential invasion for the past 75 years and so did not need Ukraine to wake it up to the danger.[12] Nonetheless, the Ukraine war has reinforced or underlined several points.

Most notably, Ukraine had eight years, starting from the annexation of Crimea and seizure of the eastern Donbas provinces in 2014, in which to put its military and society on to a war footing. To call this, as some do, 'whole-of-society resilience' may be an exaggeration but such resilience has played a vital role since the invasion commenced.[13] Despite its extensive military preparations, Taiwan has been reluctant to prioritise civil defence and has even – until 2023 – reduced the period of conscription to a bare minimum. The worked example of Ukrainian resistance should encourage Taiwan to make civil preparation more publicly apparent, which could have a deterrent effect by convincing China that a conflict could not succeed rapidly.

Furthermore, it is now even clearer than it already was that military and intelligence preparations need to be focused on protecting Taiwan's leadership from a lightning attack from the air and from infiltrated forces, both for its own sake and in order to buy time for external military support to arrive.

Finally, working to strengthen, clarify and diffuse Taiwan's competing narrative about why it deserves support, how it is determined to defend itself, and the positive contribution a free Taiwan can make both to neighbours and the wider world will play an important role in convincing other governments and their publics to help the island and oppose the invader or coercer in a time of crisis. This has, of course, long been understood, but Ukraine has underlined the need to keep emphasising and even reinventing these messages.

Specific implications for the United States

As the principal external party in any potential conflict over Taiwan, the implications of the war in Ukraine for the United States' conduct towards the island are all-encompassing. Yet it is worth underlining the fact that the clarity and credibility of America's pledges about its conduct in the event of an attempted invasion or coercion of Taiwan stand to play far and away the most decisive role in deterrence. Russia's confidence that it would not be fighting NATO forces directly in Ukraine was crucial in Putin's decision to invade. In turn, expectations amongst allies, especially those in the region, about America's involvement will determine their willingness not just to expend blood and treasure directly at the time of a crisis but also to put them at risk in advance through forward deployments and investments.

The expected speed of American military involvement is the second-most important factor in that calculus. An assumption that it could take weeks or months for US forces to arrive in the conflict theatre in sufficient numbers to make a difference could act as an encouragement to invade; conversely, an assumption that US forces, and those of allies such as Japan and Australia, would be in the theatre swiftly could act as a deterrent. The balance of that assumption is likely to evolve over time, as planned investments and deployments come slowly into place.

In summary, the lessons of Ukraine for Taiwan and the Indo-Pacific are that political decisions will play the key role, that forward deployment of outside forces will be critical for deterrence, that sanctions are irrelevant to the deterrence of major aggression, that establishment of escalation dominance will be crucial, that the speed of decision-making and delivery of outside intervention is an unpredictable variable, that the determination of the Taiwanese themselves will affect that delivery, that the battle of narratives will play a central part, and that nuclear escalation cannot be ruled out. Of course, the eventual outcome in Ukraine will likely provide further lessons and implications.

Most of all, however, the reality of the Indo-Pacific and of the prospects of conflict between the US and China is that neither the lessons nor the analysis can produce simple conclusions about deterrence. No one thought either the theory or the practice of nuclear deterrence during the Cold War was simple. But looking now at the task of deterrence, the subject looks even more like a multidimensional, multiplayer chess game. The next chapter will explore the rules and principles that might apply to such a game in the Indo-Pacific.

CHAPTER THREE

Yardsticks for deterrence

During the Cold War, deterrence became a necessary if rather distasteful concept. The apparent clarity and stability of the confrontation between the Soviet Union and the United States-led West in an almost bipolar era of nuclear weapons made the notion of mutually assured destruction (MAD) surprisingly reassuring, at least after the nuclear powers had stared into the abyss during the Cuban Missile Crisis of 1962. The principal difficulty with the idea of deterrence – that of the need to assume some sort of rationality in the decision-making of the adversary – could be overcome by virtue of the catastrophic potential involved in a nuclear exchange. However unreasonable the adversary might be in countless other ways, and however much it might operate in a framework of thinking about interests and objectives that seemed utterly different to your own, when contemplating such catastrophic consequences, the two sides clearly seemed to share common ground.

Now, more than three decades since the Cold War ended, deterrence has seemingly become a nicer if somewhat looser concept.[1] The term no longer chiefly brings to mind threats of mutual and thus planetary destruction, threats perhaps popularly associated with Dr Strangelove-like figures. The currently preferred American phrase of 'integrated deterrence' implies a unity of disparate means or domains rather than just the nuclear threat, and a collaboration between nations in the cause of peace, which again is unlikely to brook much disapproval, except among those whose aspirations to use force are thereby encumbered.[2]

The trouble is that being nicer does not make a strategic concept such as deterrence likelier to succeed. In fact, recent experience of the Ukraine war and of others that preceded it suggests that amid today's more fluid great-power rivalry, the concept needs to be thought about and applied with greater care than the often-loose use of the term implies.

In his 2004 book *Deterrence*, Lawrence Freedman writes that 'deterrence can be a technique, a doctrine and a state of mind. In all cases it is about setting boundaries for actions and establishing the risks associated with the crossing of those boundaries.'[3] It is conventionally argued that such boundaries can be set in one of two ways: by 'denial', which means convincing the adversary that your forces are capable of preventing it from achieving its aims; or by 'punishment', which involves the making of credible threats that if the boundaries are crossed then the adversary will be hit with such severe repercussions as to make the action not worthwhile.

Both definitions, however, raise the same questions: which actions, which boundaries? And how can the threat of denial or punishment truly be made credible (and sufficient) in the minds of those contemplating taking the undesired actions?

A world in flux

Clearly, the idea that the Cold War world was stable and bipolar is an oversimplification. While many countries did make enduring choices about which side they were on – by which is meant they established strong political, security and economic ties with either the Soviet Union or the West – there was also the so-called Non-Aligned Movement, consisting chiefly of many former European colonies that resisted picking sides and consequently maintained some connections to both. There was also some active and bloody competition for the allegiance of actively or passively non-aligned countries, notably the Indochina wars and many African and Latin American civil wars.

Moreover, while the Cold War can be (and was) seen as bipolar in terms of military – especially nuclear – power, the period was much more multidimensional than that military prism implies. Economic power was becoming more dispersed as Western Europe, Japan and then other parts of East Asia flourished, and democracy, the rule of law and associated culture spread and influenced the narrative of the ideological contest that the Cold War had had at its outset.

Superficially, today's world can be made to look like the simplified picture of the Cold War, with some countries clearly on either the Western or the Russo-Chinese side but most seeking to avoid making a choice and trying to maintain ties with both. However, there is a crucial difference: during the US–Soviet stand-off, the two superpowers were clearly dominant above all others in military terms, especially because of their nuclear arsenals, with China the only potentially significant disruptor of bipolarity. Both formed alliances that proved to be stable, and at the outset of the Cold War both were dominant in economic and industrial terms too, for they were the two main victors of the Second World War. Meanwhile, most of the non-aligned countries were economically and politically weak and highly internally focused, particularly those that had become newly independent after centuries of colonial rule.

In the 2020s, the now larger group of non-aligned countries is far more powerful, more outward looking and more globally engaged than were its Cold War equivalents. The US and China do have the world's two most powerful military forces and the two largest economies, but that does not make them as dominant as the US and Soviet Union looked in 1950, say, before it became evident that Japan and Western Europe were destined to become economic superpowers. While China's rise over the past half-century has been transformative and disruptive, many other countries, large and small, have also been gaining strength and some, in Asia in particular, now look capable of doing so at a faster pace than China in the coming decades.

From the point of view of deterrence, this means that seeking to achieve influence or shaping adversaries' decisions by means of the weight of partnerships or, to use another metaphor, the size of camps, must be considered uncertain of influence or success, unless those partnerships involve binding or at least highly credible commitments. To change the metaphor yet again, when the music stops you may not know who your partners will end up being.

Rationality without MADness

A key element of deterrence is the effort to understand, and then influence, the thinking and behaviour of your adversary regarding the action you are seeking to deter. Every history of the Cold War shows that both sides found doing so far from straightforward. The era was rife with misunderstandings and miscalculations. Yet the prospect of mutual annihilation in the event of a nuclear exchange produced sufficient clarity to reduce the significance of those misunderstandings and limit the scope of miscalculations.

That is not the way things look today – and it is the way things look that is central to deterrence at any given moment. Nor is this what the experience of Ukraine implies, given how Russia's nuclear threats sat alongside its conventional military aggression. Most notably, the simplest and in some ways most obvious question of all is subject to differing perceptions and thus risks a fundamental and destructive misunderstanding: is a potential Taiwan conflict to be thought of as a local, or at best regional issue? Or is it, and would it inevitably be, the centrepiece of a larger, protracted and potentially escalatory US–China war? One set of leaders, in any of Beijing, Washington or Taipei, might rationally think of it as isolatable and take actions accordingly, while others see it differently.

Deterrence is all about the psychology of leaders and of the groups around them, and the forces that are at play on those leaders at any given time. At every point in the deterrence equation – or perhaps it should be seen as a deterrence supply chain – there are different leaders, changing posts at different times, and defining different priorities. Any assessment of the strength or staying power of any strategy of deterrence in the Indo-Pacific can only ever be contingent on the nature of the moment and on the leaders who are involved at that time, on all sides.

An unstable status quo

The appeal of deterrence, particularly to those who are not direct adversaries in a binary conflict, is that it appears to represent continuity and the prevention of any change to the status quo through military means. Some such rather loose formula appears in most statements about Taiwan by countries other than China: they take no position on Taiwan's sovereignty but express their opposition to any change to the status quo by force.

One of the biggest difficulties in applying the concept of deterrence to the potential for conflict in the Indo-Pacific is rather fundamental: what is the status quo participants are trying to preserve through their deterrence?

China does not agree with even the loose definition of the status quo held by most neighbouring countries or by the West. Its view is that the status quo is defined by an expectation that unification is the agreed goal, for under its 'One China' principle the dispute is about regimes, not territory, as Taiwan is part of China. This is often conveniently conflated in Chinese statements with other states' One China policies, which for the most part are intended to leave the issue of territory to one side.

Accordingly, US and Chinese understandings of what One China means differ. They have agreed since the 1972 US–China Joint Communiqué that there is only one legitimate government of China, not two rival governments as had been implied by US diplomatic recognition of the Republic of China.[4] But they differ on whether this means that the island of Taiwan must form part of that One China: the Americans have sought to avoid taking an official position on this point.

Which brings us back to the question of what, in those circumstances, assurance can mean. Does it simply mean (as now, in the American formulation) assuring China that the US does not support and will not encourage Taiwanese independence? Or does it also need to involve assuring China that Taiwan will return to the negotiating table?

Yardsticks for Indo-Pacific deterrence

What these complexities mean is that it is even more difficult than it looks to create and apply a strategy of deterrence in the Indo-Pacific. Nonetheless, if we combine these complexities with the recent lessons from Russia and Ukraine, it is possible to define some yardsticks to be used in measuring the chances of deterrence strategies succeeding. Four such yardsticks look especially important:

1. Political will: consistency and clarity of deterrence messages
A strategy of deterrence cannot just be about possessing the military capabilities to prevent your adversary from achieving the goal you wish to obstruct. This may be necessary, but to

have a chance of also being sufficient it additionally requires evidence of the political will to use those capabilities – not just at a given moment or by a particular political leader, but a political will that can credibly be expected to be shared by successors. And that political will needs to be conveyed in clear, regular messages that the adversary will understand.

2. Military capability: speed and scale of response

To have a chance of deterring a specific action, military capabilities need not just to be adequate to prevail in an overall state-to-state conflict, should one ensue. They also need to be positioned in such a way as to be able to intervene with sufficient speed and force to alter the calculations of that adversary about the likelihood of achieving a quick victory or of denying your own aspirations. A perception by the adversary that the speed and scale of response will not, for political reasons, or cannot, for logistical reasons, be adequate would risk acting as an incentive rather than a deterrent.

3. Coalition credibility: assurance of allies and partners

These requirements for consistency and speed look particularly important for the potential role of allies and partners in the Indo-Pacific. If the active participation of countries such as Australia, Japan and the Philippines in deterrence is to remain important for Western strategy in the long term, those countries also need to be assured through consistent messages about the strategy and political will of their lead partner, the US. Otherwise, their own political will is likely to waver, and their willingness to make investments in military capabilities and infrastructure may also be placed in doubt. If the Russo-Chinese strategic partnership ever evolves to become a military alliance, the same criteria will come to apply.

4. Messaging: clarity of narrative

For all parties to the potential conflict, the need to maintain public support in their own countries, especially in a time of crisis, and the need to gain support or at least acceptance by other countries, especially those in the Indo-Pacific region itself, makes the task of defining and regularly reinforcing a clear narrative essential. Otherwise, doubts will emerge concerning the country's real reactions and likely actions in a moment of crisis, and support for whatever position that country takes will be weakened. Ideally, that narrative needs to encompass the definition of the status quo, the objectives of any potential conflict, and the military, political, moral and psychological stakes that are involved. The narrative battle over Taiwan has been under way for decades, but that does not mean that the terms have been set, still less agreed. And the associated battle of narratives about the political, social and moral characteristics of the US, the West and China, and about their respective long-term objectives, is likely to play as big a role in this contest as the equivalent battle did during the Cold War.

Let us now use these yardsticks to measure and evaluate the potential effectiveness now and in the future of the deterrence strategies we currently see in the Indo-Pacific. The natural place to start is in the US itself, since it is the progenitor of integrated deterrence.

CHAPTER FOUR

Consistent America, inconstant America

In 1987, a year that turned out to be close to the end of the four-decade Cold War between the United States and the Soviet Union, the American historian John Lewis Gaddis published a book called *The Long Peace*.[1] At the time, some considered that title a surprising phrase to describe a period of superpower confrontation during which there had been major conflicts, most notably the Korean and Vietnam wars. What he was arguing, however, was that despite those and other wars, the Cold War was a long period without a direct conflict between the great powers, in sharp contrast to the previous half-century or more. Nuclear weapons, he argued, provided a large part of the explanation.

Alongside or associated with that explanation, however, was what in hindsight looks like a notable consistency in the basic framework of US foreign and security policy towards its principal adversary: using a strategy of containment but also eventually constructing an overall system of interaction and negotiation – a consistency that the Soviet Union ultimately matched. At least from the early 1960s onwards, US presidents came and went, as did general secretaries of the Communist Party of the Soviet Union, but the basic framework remained the same, and, crucially, the main elements of the framework were clear to both sides.

Looking at American politics now, two features stand out. One is the increased polarisation between the Republican and Democratic parties, or, to label it more broadly, between conservative voters and activists on one side, and their liberal or progressive opponents on the other. The era of bipartisanship, it is commonly said, is well and truly over. Yet the second feature pushes in the opposite direction: the one issue on which there is a strong bipartisan consensus is that of China. Republicans and Democrats alike believe that the most crucial, and most potentially dangerous, confrontation that the US faces is that with China.

At times this consensus seems to feed on itself. During the presidency of Donald Trump (2017–21), a phrase in common use was 'Trump derangement syndrome', a malady identified by those who wished to argue that whatever president Trump's actual failings, too many critics were attributing almost any problem they could think of to Trump. Now there seems to be a phenomenon that could be called 'China derangement syndrome', a malady according to which almost anything that ails America may be blamed on China.

That syndrome will wax and wane according to circumstance, but it is nevertheless clear that a central core of policy towards China has become bipartisan. The Trump administration introduced a 25% import tariff on a large swathe of goods from China in 2018. The Biden administration has maintained this against the advice of many economists who point out that the tariff has merely diverted trade to other exporters, often with the involvement of Chinese companies, and has done nothing to alter America's overall trade deficit.[2]

More crucially, the Biden administration has strengthened and extended export controls on high-technology goods and equipment that were first introduced by the Trump administration, notably for advanced semiconductors and the equipment required to manufacture them.[3] The general tariffs represent a bipartisan consensus that America should be tough on China and offer no concessions unless China changes its behaviour; the technology controls represent a consensus that any means available should be used to slow the technological advancement of the Chinese military, for that advancement risks threatening the national security of the US and its allies.

The most important continuity of all can be seen in an American strategy of shifting more military power to the Indo-Pacific, deploying it in new ways that are more attuned to the requirements of deterrence, and building up a network of alliances and partnerships dedicated to stronger military capacity and deterrence. This was first labelled as 'the pivot to Asia' under Barack Obama's administration, and was given new impetus and a greater focus during the Trump administration – chiefly under the initiative of Matt Pottinger, the National Security Council's (NSC) senior director for Asia, as well as successive secretaries of defense.[4] It achieved a further fruition during the Biden administration under the leadership of Kurt Campbell, first at the NSC and then as deputy secretary of state. Campbell had also been involved in the Obama administration's 'pivot'.

Two examples of that continuity can be seen in America's evolving relationships with Japan and India. Japan and the US first began to talk seriously about building up Japan's military strength and role in the Indo-Pacific two decades ago when Koizumi Junichiro was prime minister of Japan in 2001–06. Both countries were becoming conscious of China's rising power and hostile behaviour, as well as of the nuclear threat posed by its semi-associate, North Korea. The main progenitor of Japan's military transformation, however, was Abe Shinzo, thanks to his holding the prime ministership for eight consecutive years

(2012–20) and thereby establishing collaborative relationships with both presidents Obama and Trump. The course begun by Koizumi and then defined and shaped by Abe reached its at-least-interim destination with the plans published by Abe's successor-but-one, Kishida Fumio, to increase defence spending by about 60% in 2023–27 and to take a much fuller part in the deterrence strategy of Japan's security-treaty ally, the US. Chapter Seven will discuss this in more detail.

Abe was keen even during his first, ill-fated, period in office (2006–07) to establish a new so-called Quadrilateral Security Dialogue (the Quad) with Australia, India and the US so as to draw India into security conversations with Western powers. The idea did not fly at that time, but was revived by Trump in agreement with Abe, and then actually implemented by Joe Biden. This had followed more than 20 years of efforts by both America and Japan to court India, starting in the early 2000s with Japanese-financed infrastructure projects, and then a US–India civil nuclear-power agreement struck by president George W. Bush in 2005.[5] All these efforts by successive Japanese prime ministers and US presidents have had a common goal: to ensure that India could become a counterbalance to Chinese power in the Indo-Pacific or, to put it more minimally, to ensure that India does not become dependent on or too close to China.

Political will: consistency and clarity of deterrence messages

At this general level of China policy, then, recent American approaches have been consistent, have consistently become tougher and are likely to remain so. However, for the specific task of deterring China from using military force to attempt to capture or coerce Taiwan, different sorts of policy consistency are required. Three are likely to matter:

- A consistent and well-broadcast political and military resolve showing the willingness to go to war to defend Taiwan.

- A consistent willingness to deploy military forces in a manner that indicates that if intervention is ordered it will be speedy and highly material, and a related willingness to invest in and support alliance partners to encourage them to do the same.
- A consistent and well-communicated foreign policy towards China that determines whether America is to be considered by the People's Republic of China (PRC) and other countries in the region as a provocative crosser of Chinese red lines and breacher of past agreements, or as an assurer over the issue of Taiwanese independence. Put another way, a foreign policy that positions America clearly as a power favouring the status quo rather than one seeking to change it.

For all the bipartisan consensus concerning China in general, these sorts of consistency around deterrence currently look more elusive than did the policy consistency of the Cold War. Consider the following four quotations, all from the past five years:

- **President Donald Trump, 2019**, in reported comments to an unnamed senator: 'Taiwan is like two feet from China. We are eight thousand miles away. If they invade there isn't a fucking thing we can do about it.'[6]
- **Mike Pompeo, formerly Trump's US secretary of state, March 2022**, in a speech in Taipei: 'The United States government should immediately take necessary and long overdue steps to do the right and obvious thing which is to offer the Republic of China (Taiwan) America's diplomatic recognition as a free and sovereign country.'[7]
- **President Joe Biden, May 2022**, as reported by the Associated Press and others: 'Biden, at a news conference in Tokyo, said "yes" when asked if he was willing to get involved militarily to defend Taiwan if China invaded. "That's the commitment we made", he added.'[8]

- **Former president Donald Trump, July 2023**, in a Fox News TV interview, on semiconductors: 'Taiwan, they took our business away. We should have stopped them. We should have taxed them. We should have tariffed them.'[9]

We could debate the merits of any of those statements: whether Biden's pledge is credible; whether Trump really said that to a senator and if so whether it is really what he thinks; whether Trump's semiconductors claim, made once he was out of office, really implies that in office he or a like-minded successor would punish Taiwan economically; whether the views of a former secretary of state (and former director of the CIA) when out of office are indicative of what the Republican Party he belongs to thinks, or whether he would hold those views if he were to gain public office again.

What we cannot say is that the messages America's political leaders have been sending are unified or consistent. In the case of the speech by former secretary of state Pompeo, his remarks contradict the basic texts of agreements between the US and China, and between the US and Taiwan that have governed relations since 1972. Those remarks positioned America as a revisionist power, not a status quo one.[10]

During the Cold War there were many conflicting messages about American thinking, whether among intellectuals or policymakers. But once the post-Cuban Missile Crisis frameworks had been put in place, there was still a basic consistency about the messages that were most relevant to deterrence. As far as we know, at no point following 1962 was the Soviet leadership seriously tempted to consider military action against the US or in Washington's immediate neighbourhood by a perception that a new president or their national-security team had a markedly different view to those held by their predecessors.

In contrast, the range of views expressed currently concerning Taiwan and China, even within a generally bipartisan consensus, poses a risk for a deterrence strategy. The risk is threefold. Firstly, implying that a change of administration could lead to a change of political will or policy could encourage opportunism, whether mistakenly or otherwise. Secondly, implying that new thinking is taking hold about the One China policy or Taiwan's status could act as a provocation. Thirdly, blurring the narrative about Taiwan itself and its economic and political behaviour could undermine domestic public and political support for any military intervention, thereby reducing the credibility of a deterrent threat, and erode support or acquiescence within the Indo-Pacific region for intervention or for building an intervention capability.

Military capability and coalition credibility

From the point of view of the US military, a mission of deterrence has two main purposes: deterring conflict, chiefly by influencing the psychology of the adversary; and ensuring that, if deterrence fails, the armed forces are capable of winning whatever conflict may ensue.

The second part of that mission concerns the overall balance of military, industrial and technological capabilities, including nuclear arsenals, and is a long-term task. But much of the immediate military and diplomatic work will go towards the first part, that of influencing psychology. The intent must be to raise serious doubts in the minds of Chinese military planners and political decision-makers about whether the chances of an invasion succeeding or a blockade being maintained are high enough to make the attempt worthwhile. On the other hand, the goal of US military strategists will also be to ensure that US political decision-makers believe they stand a chance of stopping it, if the decision to intervene were to be made. In this sort of evaluation, the most important elements are likely to be geography and time. Coalition credibility is also an important factor here, for the level of active support from Japan, the Philippines and Australia in particular will affect both geography and time in critical ways. Chapters Seven and Eight will address this in detail.

Russia's 2022 invasion of Ukraine showed that an invader can succeed in convincing themselves that their superiority over the immediate adversary is so great that they will make such rapid progress as to be able to bring the issue to a close before outside powers have had time to take their decisions and to move their forces into the theatre – a 'fait accompli'. Rapid success in the case of Taiwan would then place the burden of escalation on those outside forces, obliging them to decide whether they wish to take on the costs of challenging that success through their own invasion or blockade to liberate the island, and whether they will be able to persuade their own public to support them in doing so.

That is why an important military yardstick is that of speed, both of decision-making and of response, combined with scale. For deterrence to have a chance of working, the expected pace of decision-making and response must be sufficiently and credibly rapid, and at a sufficient scale to be able to affect the psychology of the adversary.

If we examine the threat from North Korea, America measures up well on this yardstick. Ever since the Korean War of 1950–53, it has kept military forces near the border in South Korea (currently 28,500 spread across multiple bases), whom the North Koreans would expect to respond rapidly to any attack, and it has kept air bases in neighbouring Japan from which its fighters and bombers could reach the Korean Peninsula within minutes.[11] There is little reason to doubt that America's long-standing policy of 'extended deterrence' – bringing its treaty allies under its nuclear umbrella – applies to the Korean Peninsula. Although there has been some public debate in South Korea about whether the country should start its own nuclear-weapons programme as a hedge against American unreliability, the government's conclusion has been rather as it was in the 1970s when the country abandoned a secret nuclear programme: that it is far better to keep US conventional forces in the peninsula and to rely on US extended deterrence than to risk America deciding that South Korea no longer needed its help.[12]

Taiwan is a more difficult challenge, as Trump's reported (but unconfirmed) 2019 comment acknowledged. Since the withdrawal of US bases from Taiwan in 1979 and from the Philippines in 1992, the United States' nearest bases for the US Air Force and US Marine Corps have been on the Japanese island of Okinawa, which is close but still 350 nautical miles from Taiwan. The home of the US Seventh Fleet is Yokosuka in Tokyo Bay on the Japanese main island, which is over 1,100 nm from Taiwan, although the Seventh Fleet also shares a naval base with the Japan Maritime Self-Defense Force (JMSDF) at Sasebo, near Nagasaki on the island of Kyushu, which is 650 nm from Taiwan.

The development by China of strong anti-access/area denial (commonly abbreviated as A2/AD) capabilities, by means chiefly of missiles and submarines, has made it harder for the US to rely, as it did during the Taiwan Strait Crisis of 1996, on displaying and projecting power simply by sailing carrier strike groups into the area, or by using airpower. A naval force would anyway take some time to arrive unless it happened to be nearby, or unless intelligence about Chinese preparations had led it to be dispatched in anticipation: sailing time from Yokosuka, for a carrier strike group to a position 350 nm off Taiwan's east coast, placing it in range to enter combat, would be one day, 16 hours, or two days, 12 hours if support ships were also needed.[13] From Okinawa it would be 14 hours. Sailing time at 20 knots from Hawaii would be nine days; from San Diego, home port of the majority of the US Pacific Fleet, it would be 12 days, 12 hours. A *Virginia*-class nuclear submarine based in Perth, Western Australia, would take four days, 21 hours to reach that same area, sailing at 28 knots submerged.

For this reason, the US Department of Defense has been announcing and implementing a series of redeployments designed to show that in the case of an invasion or blockade of Taiwan, US forces would be able to respond more quickly and at greater scale than those sailing times appear to indicate – that is, sufficiently quickly and effectively to act as a deterrent. And some of those changes in force posture have also been designed to mitigate the problem of A2/AD: that if China were to choose to make pre-emptive missile strikes on US and allied bases – thereby making a de facto declaration of war, however – the fixed and not always adequately resilient air bases on Okinawa and the Korean Peninsula would be vulnerable.

These redeployments also look intended to reverse the impression given by the 'realignment' agreed in 2006 between the US and Japan under which the US was pulling some forces further away from the theatre.[14] Following that agreement, in 2012 Japan and the US decided that 9,000 of the 19,000 marines then in Okinawa would be moved far further away, to Guam and Hawaii. This was in response to local Okinawan criticism of the size and impact of the US presence on that island, opposition that has been building for decades. That realignment has taken time, because of the need to build new bases, but is finally happening, albeit still gradually. In 2024, 1,300 US marines will move from Okinawa to the new Camp Blaz on Guam, to be joined by 3,700 personnel filled on a rotational basis from the US.[15]

The broader posture and reconfiguration were laid out in the 2018 National Defense Strategy and are labelled as 'Dynamic Force Employment'.[16] The essence of this approach – seeking greater unpredictability in basing and the rotation of forces between a wider range of options – is not new: for example, the US Marine Corps has had a 'Marine Rotational Force' in Darwin, Australia, since 2012. But a spate of recent announcements has reinforced the process and given the impression that it is accelerating. These include, but are not limited to:

1. The redesignation of the 12th Marine Regiment in Okinawa as the 12th Marine Littoral Regiment in November 2023. This designation indicates an expeditionary regiment equipped and trained to act in an even nimbler but still forceful way. This is the first such Marine Littoral Regiment to be deployed in Okinawa or the first island chain, and it adds to the 3rd Marine Littoral Regiment in Hawaii, which was similarly redesignated in 2022. Thus, there will be fewer marines on Okinawa, but the remaining ones will be more geared to respond to an invasion or blockade of Taiwan.[17]
2. The establishment of a Composite Watercraft Company in Yokohama, Japan, in 2023, bringing with it 13 transport vessels.[18] Again, this is intended to make US forces look and be more manoeuvrable.
3. The withdrawal of two F-15 *Eagle* fighter squadrons from Okinawa in December 2022 and their replacement by a rotational force of more advanced F-22 *Raptor* stealth fighters.[19]
4. The transfer, announced in October 2023, of a squadron of MQ-9 *Reaper* drones from the JMSDF Kanoya Air Base in Kyushu (the southernmost of Japan's four main islands) to the Kadena Air Base in Okinawa. This is the 319th Expeditionary Reconnaissance Squadron,

consisting of eight *Reapers*. Although these uninhabited aircraft are primarily for surveillance, the move to a US base will also make it more politically acceptable for the drones to be equipped with missiles and bombs.[20]

5. A temporary expansion by the US Navy in 2022 of the number of *Los Angeles*-class fast-attack nuclear-propelled submarines operating from a base in Guam from four to five, and more crucially, the expansion of maintenance and training facilities on the island in the next decade.[21] An important element of the US forces' response to China's A2/AD capabilities lies under the sea, in the form of submarines. These *Los Angeles*-class submarines are equipped chiefly with *Tomahawk* land-attack cruise missiles (LACMs).

6. The establishment of the Submarine Rotational Force–West, to consist of one British submarine and 'up to four' US *Virginia*-class submarines, which will start 'rotating' through HMAS Stirling in Perth, Western Australia, 'as early as 2027', under the AUKUS deal between Australia, the United Kingdom and the US, in addition to building nuclear-propelled submarines for entry into service in the Royal Australian Navy in the 2030s and 2040s.[22] This means the force will visit, will use that Australian base and will start training Australian submariners, but will not sit there permanently. Crucially these submarine fleets in Guam and Perth will spend large amounts of time at sea in the Pacific, including the South China and East China seas.

7. The enhancement of ballistic-missile capabilities. The demise in 2019 of the Intermediate-Range Nuclear Forces (INF) Treaty between the US and Russia has enabled the US to seek to match Chinese ballistic-missile capabilities.[23] As an IISS Research Paper stated in January 2024, the US

is now developing faster, longer-range systems, such as the air-launched Hypersonic Attack Cruise Missile, the naval Conventional Prompt Strike (CPS) system and the ground-launched Long-Range Hypersonic Weapon known as *Dark Eagle*, for deployment in the mid-2020s.[24] In the meantime, ground-launched *Tomahawk* LACMs could somewhat fill the gap. Basing is a problem, however, as so far none of the United States' regional allies – Japan, the Philippines, South Korea or, further afield, Australia – have agreed to allow such long-range US missiles to be located on their territories. Pending any such agreement, Guam is the likeliest base, with the CPS system also being deployed on ships and submarines.

8. The establishment of base and logistics facilities in the Philippines, under the so-called Enhanced Defense Cooperation Agreement between that country and the US first signed in 2014 but accelerated since 2021, which will be described in more detail in Chapter Eight.[25] These nine sites allow the US to build infrastructure for storage of fuel and ammunition as well as runways and command-and-control facilities, and for joint training with Philippine forces. In the event of a conflict, it would be up to the Philippines to decide whether to allow US forces to use these facilities, but if it does this would greatly assist the US military to move and be re-equipped nimbly.

9. Japan's own force redeployment, under the new National Security Strategy and Defense Buildup Programme announced in 2022.[26] That redeployment is designed to strengthen Japan's defence of its most southwestern islands, the so-called Nansei chain that runs southwest of Okinawa and represents the closest islands to Taiwan. Chapter Seven will look at this in more detail, but in summary the plans are for Japan to locate anti-ship missile

batteries in the southwest islands as well as electronic-surveillance and warfare facilities. Provided the US and Japan continue to see eye to eye, this will provide US forces both with well-placed support in the event of a conflict and with further options for the supply and basing of their own forces.

Is this force posture likely to look speedy enough and threatening enough to act as a strong deterrent? Much depends on whether China would contemplate embarking on a full-scale war right from the start, by making pre-emptive missile attacks on US and Japanese bases so as to neutralise that deterrent, or whether it would prefer the option of making a rapid assault on Taiwan, or setting up a blockade, daring the US to escalate and gambling that it could establish enough of a fait accompli to persuade the US to back down.

The perceived speed and nimbleness of the United States' initial force posture will be important in shaping that bet. Bearing in mind the impact of the US–Japan Roadmap for Realignment, moving some forces back from Okinawa to Guam and Hawaii, and the fact that the largest concentrations of US forces at bases in Japan and South Korea remain vulnerable to missile attack, the verdict has to be that while this adjusted force posture is undoubtedly helpful, more will need to be done. Consistency and predictability of the US response is the primary factor determining the effectiveness of its deterrent, but speed and nimbleness come an important second.

The narrative yardstick

The final yardstick for America's deterrence strategy that needs to be evaluated is that of clarity of narrative. This breaks into two parts: firstly, the narrative about why Taiwan and its freedom matters to America, a narrative that is important for domestic public opinion and for America's allies and partners; and secondly, the narrative about the One China policy the US has followed since 1972 and what it means today for policy towards both China and Taiwan.

The very nature of the Taiwan situation – that of a permanent anomaly in world affairs and an unresolved legacy of the Second World War as well as of China's civil war and the First Sino-Japanese War of 1895 – makes it hard to maintain a clear and persuasive narrative. Is this island of 23.4 million people, 'eight thousand miles away', as Trump reportedly said, worth fighting a war over? Various answers to that question have been current at various times.

The two principal public arguments used today in the US are that Taiwan is a flourishing democracy, one whose freedoms are worth defending and to whom the US has made commitments; and that Taiwan is vital as a producer of the most sophisticated semiconductors – by some measures, production in Taiwan supplies 80% of world demand for such high-end chips, though it all depends on what is defined as 'high-end' – making it important that such technology be part of the free world rather than controlled by one country, China.[27]

The arguments used in policy circles are somewhat different. The main one, as laid out in Chapter One, emphasises the strategic importance of Taiwan for control of some of the busiest shipping lanes in the world and, critically, of the South China and East China seas. Keeping Taiwan out of any single power's control therefore averts the danger that that single power – China – might in future seek to use that control to coerce regional nations, including US allies Japan, the Philippines and South Korea. On this argument, Taiwan matters because control of the region matters, and because China's likely intentions in using that control would be malign and contrary to US interests.

The second argument is one based on principles about opposing the use of force to settle international disputes and in particular to alter borders, and on the fact that in the three US–China Joint Communiqués (1972, 1979 and 1982) China agreed that neither country 'should seek hegemony in the Asia-Pacific region' and that both would 'strive for a peaceful solution' to the Taiwan question.[28] China's establishment of military bases on reclaimed reefs and islands in the South China Sea, and its strengthened emphasis on its supposed historic claims to that sea, already can be said to represent a breach of that promise by 'seeking hegemony'. A Chinese invasion of Taiwan or coerced unification would, it is argued, be an unacceptable use of force and would be an explicit effort to achieve hegemony.

Of all these arguments, the weakest – or least likely to remain convincing over time – is the one based on Taiwan's technological importance. Known in Taiwan itself as 'the Silicon Shield', it is unconvincing because it feels excessively transactional and depends on untestable assumptions that after a war, trade in this technology would not simply resume and that adaptation to any 'loss' of free Taiwan would not be possible. Taiwan's leading producer, the Taiwan Semiconductor Manufacturing Company (TSMC), is already making huge investments in semiconductor fabs (factories) in Europe, Japan and the US, which in coming years will make chip users less dependent on Taiwan for their supplies.[29] These new fabs will not make the most high-end chips, but to base a war on ensuring the continued availability of some advanced semiconductors – a product few people can understand – will not be convincing.

Taiwan's flourishing democracy and the case for protecting its freedoms are likely to provide a more convincing argument, though that argument's saliency to US public opinion may depend on the circumstances in which it needs to be deployed: will this be a time when democracies in general look both saveable and worth saving, or might the public shrug its shoulders at the cause of protecting a faraway island the size of the state of Maryland?

In a crisis, the policy circles' arguments will, no doubt, become blended with the public ones. The American national interest in keeping the Western Pacific open and in defending long-time treaty allies against coercion or direct attack will be central. The persuasiveness of this will depend on whether the public and indeed political circles are at that moment convinced of the case for America's global interests and engagements, or whether a more isolationist mood prevails. That caveat also applies, as it has over Ukraine, to the argument about the unacceptability of the use of force to change borders or settle international disputes. Whatever the United Nations Charter may say, this is not a principle on which it is always possible to maintain consistency let alone achieve agreement.

This applies above all to the One China framework for US–China and US–Taiwan relations. Under the three US–China Joint Communiqués and the 'Six Assurances' (for Taiwan), US policy has been based uncomfortably but so far securely on a set of pledges that look less and less convincing as time passes. The three communiqués do not provide a reliable basis for future policy, whatever China might like to claim. These were solemn and binding commitments made based on things that were true at the time but no longer are. A key pledge made in the 1972 US–China Joint Communiqué was that 'the United States acknowledges that all Chinese on either side of the Taiwan Strait maintain there is but one China and that Taiwan is a part of China ... The United States Government does not challenge that position.'[30]

This made sense at a time when the authoritarian Kuomintang government of Taiwan continued to claim to be the rightful government of the whole of China. Now, half a century later, it is no longer true that 'all Chinese' on the Taiwanese side of the strait maintain this view, and that fact is regularly made plain by Taiwan's democracy and free expression.

In the 1982 US–China Joint Communiqué, the Americans maintained those commitments and added a promise about arms sales to Taiwan:

> The United States Government states that it does not seek to carry out a long-term policy of arms sales to Taiwan, that its arms sales to Taiwan will not exceed, either in qualitative or quantitative terms, the level of those supplied in recent years since the establishment of diplomatic relations between the United States and China, and that it intends to reduce gradually its sales of arms to Taiwan, leading over a period of time to a final resolution.[31]

While there is plenty of room for differing interpretations about the qualitative or quantitative measures of US arms sales to Taiwan and of whether the US has complied with that pledge, it is incontestable that, over time, the US has not gradually reduced its arms sales to Taiwan. Nor has it, since 1982, appeared to be in any sense seeking to lead towards 'a final resolution'.

Wording agreed upon four or five decades ago in very different circumstances is unlikely to be a good guide to conduct now. This highlights, however, the case for new dialogue and a new framework between the US and the PRC to clarify both sides' positions on Taiwan. Such a framework would be hard to achieve, to say the least, in the current conditions of mutual hostility, but efforts on the American side to open such a dialogue, or at least to debate what should be said, would assist in providing clarity to a narrative that has become foggy at best, contentious at worst. The most important thing America needs to keep on repeating and clarifying is that it will continue to oppose a unilateral Taiwanese declaration of independence, for this would plainly be a *casus belli* for the PRC.

The most fundamental reality, however, is that despite all the One China language, both the Chinese and the US sides know full well that most Taiwanese people oppose unification (whether peaceful or forced) and that all US governments to date have been opposed to it, too. In that rather basic sense, clarity has imposed itself on the issue. What remains unclear is what price any of the three parties – the US, China or Taiwan – is prepared to pay to achieve their preferred outcome.

CHAPTER FIVE

Taiwan and its predicament

Outsiders often voice doubts as to whether the Taiwanese people would really fight to defend their freedom. The truth is that despite years of preparation it was not certain how Ukrainians or their leaders would react either, until the reality of war descended upon them on 24 February 2022, and initial success in repelling the invader then built on itself. For a foretaste of how some young Taiwanese people, at least, think about cross-strait relations and the case for getting closer to the People's Republic of China (PRC), it is worth looking back at what happened in Taiwan in 2014, the same year as Ukraine suffered the illegal annexation of its province of Crimea by Russian forces, and when the pro-democracy 'umbrella' movement first paralysed central Hong Kong.

The story began in 2013 when the then Kuomintang (KMT) government, under then-president Ma Ying-jeou, negotiated a significant trade deal, the Cross-Strait Services Trade Agreement (CSSTA), with the PRC.[1] Despite having for decades been dedicated, in theory at least, to retaking the mainland, which its leader, General Chiang Kai-shek, and his followers left in 1949, the modern KMT stands for closer relations with the PRC. The CSSTA was aimed at serving this goal by opening large areas of service industries in Taiwan to Chinese investment, and in China to Taiwanese investment, and followed a previous agreement mainly for goods trade, the Economic Cooperation Framework Agreement, signed early in Ma's first term as president in 2010.

Facing likely public dissent over some parts of the agreement, the KMT decided to renege on an earlier deal with the opposition Democratic Progressive Party (DPP) for a detailed parliamentary review of the CSSTA and instead to push it straight to a full yes-or-no vote in the legislature. This triggered a popular rebellion, which took the form of an occupation of the Legislative Yuan (parliament) by a coalition of student and civil-society groups initially led by a student body called 'Black Island Nation Youth'. In a smart piece of political marketing, this Taiwanese rebellion later adopted the name the 'Sunflower Movement'.

It sounds extraordinary that a rather technical, business-oriented matter, the CSSTA, should give rise to a 24-day occupation of the Legislative Yuan, a substantial amendment of the legislation and ultimately a change of government. Who could object to closer economic ties with what was then the world's fastest-growing large economy? Plenty of people, was the answer, because they feared that those closer economic ties could also bring greater Chinese political influence that risked harming Taiwan's freedom of expression – notably through Chinese ownership of media groups – and thereby potentially all its other freedoms. There was also, it is true, a strong element of protest simply at what was seen as a high-handed, undemocratic way of governing by the KMT, amid suspicions that the trade agreement would really serve the KMT's friends in business rather than the wider economy. But the broad issue related to fear of Chinese influence, and ultimately domination.

The occupation did not come completely out of the blue. It followed activism in earlier years against what were seen as excessively kowtowing approaches to China by the KMT government, and against the takeover of a local media group by a pro-China Taiwanese conglomerate. It operated in parallel to a campaign against the construction of a nuclear-power plant in an area of the island known to be vulnerable to earthquakes. Moreover, no campaign that involves the occupation of a parliament and thus the obstruction of legislative work can be seen as straightforwardly pro-democratic. As Ian Rowen (an American who took part in the occupation and is now an associate professor at the National Taiwan Normal University) writes, 'a sustained civil occupation of a key government building is hard to imagine in most countries, and points simultaneously and paradoxically to Taiwan's high degrees of both political fractiousness and social civility'.[2]

The occupation was nonetheless non-violent and drew upon widespread public support and sympathy. The view that the KMT had mishandled not just the cross-strait negotiations but also the opposition to the CSSTA and the occupation went on to contribute to its defeats in mid-term local elections later in 2014 and then in presidential and legislative elections two years later.

For the present purpose, the main lessons from the Sunflower Movement are two: that Taiwanese civil society can organise itself rapidly and in a sophisticated way when the need or desire arises; and that there is considerable public concern about the potential consequences of becoming too close to China. The argument that economic ties, bringing jobs and higher incomes, will trump everything else did not work in 2014 when China was booming. It would be even less likely to work now, with the shine having gone from the Chinese economy. Economic factors still count as highly in Taiwanese elections as they do elsewhere – economic concerns largely explain why the incumbent DPP lost its parliamentary majority in the January 2024 polls to a revived KMT and an insurgent third party, the Taiwan People's Party – but the answer to the economic question is no longer closer ties with China.

The success and strength of the Sunflower Movement need to be kept in mind when trying to evaluate what is inescapably the first and main yardstick for Taiwan's own ability to deter an invasion or attempted coercion by the PRC: the resilience of its society and its willingness to put up resistance. A peaceful occupation of the parliament is rather different from a war when missiles are raining down and ships are crossing the Taiwan Strait. But it is the most recent indicator of Taiwanese society's willingness to act rather than simply to offer opinions.

Along with opinion polls, the memory of the Sunflower Movement also ensures that no Chinese political leader would reasonably believe that invading or blockading Chinese troops would be greeted by cheering crowds bearing garlands. It also helps explain why, in the final days of the January 2024 presidential-election campaign, the KMT candidate, Hou You-ih, emphasised that he did not harbour 'unrealistic thoughts about China': like his opponents, as president he said he would strengthen Taiwan's defences and had no intention of negotiating with China about unification.[3] In that campaign, although it was ultimately won by the candidate China considers most separatist, Lai Ching-te of the incumbent DPP, there was a remarkable consensus among all three candidates about defence and unification, leaving the main debate to be about jobs, housing and other socio-economic issues.

Opinion polls show clearly why such positions make sense. A poll taken twice a year since 1994 for the Election Study Center at National Chengchi University in Taipei reveals a big gap between the declining share of the population answering that they would favour either 'unification as soon as possible' (1.6% of respondents in June 2023) or 'maintain status quo, move towards unification' (5.8%), and those groups agreeing that Taiwan should 'maintain status quo indefinitely' (32.1%) or 'maintain status quo, decide at later date' (28.6%).[4] The number of people favouring a move towards independence has also declined, and only a small group (4.5%) argue for seeking independence as soon as possible (see Figure 1). But there is no sign at all of eagerness for unification, and an overwhelming preference for keeping things as they are.[5]

These attitudes can also be interpreted as indicating a preference for the avoidance of conflict, especially a war with China, but also conflict inside Taiwan. Keeping things as they are is a way of doing both, especially as the status quo has worked well for the Taiwanese population of 23.4 million, more than one-quarter of whom were born since democracy was established

Figure 1: **Changes in the unification–independence stances of Taiwanese, 1994–June 2023**

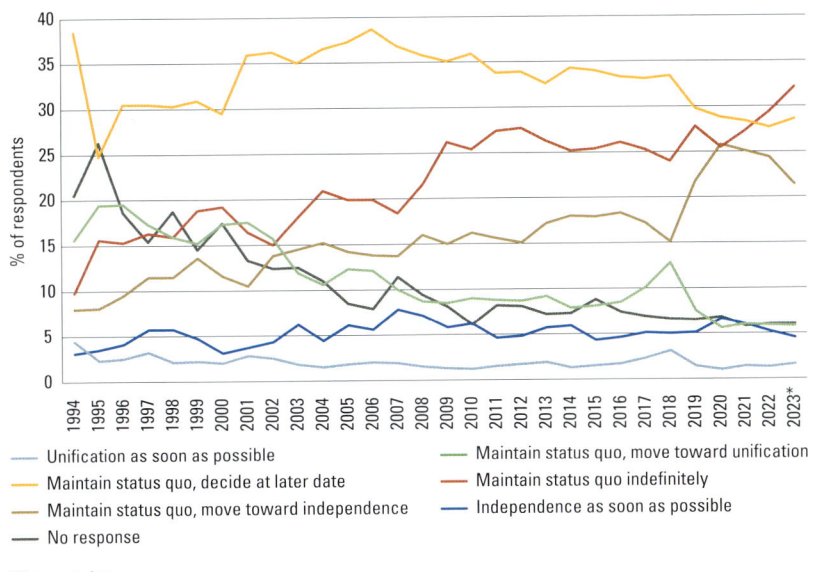

*Data up to June
Source: Election Study Center, National Chengchi University   ©IISS

in the early 1990s.[6] Not surprisingly, these attitudes correlate with polls asking whether people identify themselves as Chinese, Taiwanese or both. In a similarly long-term survey for the Election Study Center, in 2008 the proportion of respondents identifying themselves chiefly as Taiwanese overtook those identifying themselves as both Chinese and Taiwanese, and in the June 2023 poll amounted to a clearly dominant 62.8% of the population, compared with the 30.5% who still said they identified themselves as both (see Figure 2).[7] The proportion seeing themselves as principally Chinese has dropped from one-quarter in 1992 when this polling began to just 2.5% in June 2023.

The victory of Lai Ching-te of the DPP in the presidential election of 13 January 2024 means that there is no chance during the next four years of a Taiwanese government seeking to impose cross-strait negotiations, still less unification, on Taiwanese voters, and ensures that the previous DPP government's efforts at reinforcing defence will continue. In what form

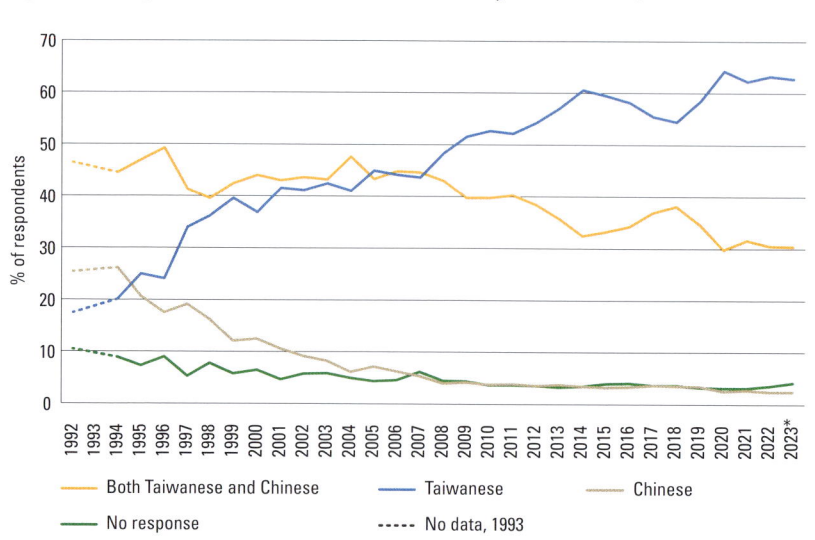

Figure 2: **Changes in the Taiwanese/Chinese identity of Taiwanese, 1992–June 2023**

*Data up to June
Source: Election Study Center, National Chengchi University   ©IISS

that happens, however, will depend on how well President Lai succeeds in working with a Legislative Yuan in which his party no longer has a working majority.

Lai, who also uses the name William Lai when meeting westerners, served as vice-president under Tsai Ing-wen in 2020–24 and is an experienced politician who tried to compete with Tsai during her first term as president in part by taking a more pro-independence stance than her. Officially he now stands for autonomy, Taiwanese identity and international respect for Taiwan rather than for formal independence, but it is certain that the Chinese leadership will consider him to be even more of a foe of unification than they did Tsai. Cross-strait talks have been suspended by the PRC since 2016, when Tsai took office.

Those talks will now surely remain suspended, and Chinese 'grey-zone' pressure through daily incursions into Taiwanese air and sea space will continue or even intensify. The task for President Lai and his new government, beyond domestic economic and social policy, will be to work towards strengthening Taiwan's own contribution to the deterrence of a Chinese invasion or blockade while also persuading the United States and its allies to maintain and reinforce their own deterrence strategies.

Taiwan's political will is not in doubt, making consistency less of an issue than in the case of the US. The questions about Taiwan's deterrence strategy narrow down to two of the yardsticks:

1. Capabilities: can it display sufficient levels of military and civil resilience, or preparedness, to convince Chinese military planners that an invasion or blockade would be far from a walkover, to increase the amount of time available for US and other forces to arrive, and to look deserving of military and diplomatic support from international partners?

2. Narrative: can it meet those yardsticks while also maintaining and communicating policies clearly and consistently enough to avoid provoking or justifying a military attempt to change the status quo?

Military resilience

Compared with the giant People's Liberation Army (PLA), the Taiwanese military is a dwarf, just as this small island, 394 kilometres long by 145 km wide, with a population of 23.4m, is a mere speck alongside China, a land mass more than 250 times larger with a population of 1.4 billion. Taiwan's annual defence budget in 2023 was US$18.6bn, a rise of 9.8% on the previous year in real terms; China's official 2023 budget was US$222.9bn, almost 12 times as big.[8]

The real question, though, is not whether tiny Taiwan could defeat mighty China. It is whether Taiwan's armed forces and civilians could hold out against a Chinese assault or blockade for long enough to make such a venture highly costly for China but also, more critically, to allow time for allies, led by the US, to send sufficient forces to the area to be able to intervene militarily and to provide supplies of essential goods. A 2023 study by the RAND Corporation defined this requirement as 'the national government's ability to oversee a resolute military defense of the island during a 90-day period from the onset of a major attack by China'. The RAND authors' verdict was that Taiwan would fail this test.[9]

Ninety days was, however, a very demanding definition. As Chapter Four sought to show, if the US is willing to carry out President Joe Biden's pledge and intervene directly, China's PLA can expect US submarines, fighters, bombers, missiles and the Marine Littoral Regiment to be engaging with Chinese forces a lot sooner than in 90 days. Ships could arrive from Japan, Guam or even San Diego within 2–12 days, though getting them there in a large force would take a bit longer. Countermoves against a blockade would also be expected to happen a lot sooner. Although US (and allied) forces are not yet ideally positioned for a rapid and nimble response, no Chinese planner will be reckoning on having three months of grace before a substantial US intervention arrives.

Nonetheless, the 'if' in the statement about American willingness to carry out Biden's pledge is a massive one. It is also conceivable that a future US president might base a decision on whether to intervene directly, and thus to escalate the conflict, at least in part on the initial political, social and military response in Taiwan itself. After all, that fits with the lesson from Ukraine: Taiwan does not only have to be strategically and morally important, it also must look as if it 'deserves' support, for support will be costly. That issue is partly military and partly social-cum-political.

On the military aspect, none of the issues about Taiwan's strategy and capabilities is new: they have formed part of defence plans throughout the past 75 years and can be seen laid out in each of the Quadrennial Defense Reviews produced by the Ministry of National Defense.[10] Nonetheless, some of the strongest doubts about the nation's resilience come from inside Taiwan itself, especially given a perception that the armed forces' traditional closeness to their long-time overlords during the authoritarian years, the KMT, has made them resistant to modernisation. Some in the DPP also wanted, especially in the early years of democracy, to keep the soldiers in their barracks and weaken them for fear that they might intervene in politics.

Three decades later, those perceptions are fading, to be replaced by fears that civilian control over military investment and procurement has been inadequate, and that training and development of the officer class of all the military services takes place too much in isolation and with service contracts that are too short. Perhaps the biggest difficulty, however, one shared with other East Asian nations suffering declining fertility and ageing populations, is recruitment and retention of military professionals as opposed to conscripts. Taiwan's population reached a peak of 23.6m in 2020, and on the latest official estimate was just over 23.4m in March 2024.[11] By mid-century it will have joined Japan, South Korea and indeed China as a super-aged society.

Much American criticism, by contrast, focuses on an alleged Taiwanese military preference for shiny and costly platforms such as warships and fighter jets that such critics argue would be likely to be destroyed swiftly in the event of a war. This overlooks the fact that until a war happens, the main activity of the nation's navy and air force has to be one of responding to grey-zone incursions. As Figure 3 shows, these incursions have become frequent.

Nonetheless, even from inside the US Department of Defense, the main pressure-cum-advice being given to Taiwan in recent years, especially since the invasion of Ukraine, has been that it should build up its ability to fight an 'asymmetric' war using missiles, drones, and air and sea defences to fend off and slow down an invasion. There is not, however, a black-and-white choice between being asymmetric or conventional: to deal with the circumstances Taiwan finds itself in requires it to be both. Being a 'porcupine' using stocks of shoulder-launched missiles, *Patriot* missile batteries and automatic rifles as your spines will make good sense if an invasion is ever attempted, but other military assets are also needed, whether in normal times or times of war, ideally ones that can serve both purposes while placing doubts in the mind of the adversary.

That is why one of the main defence debates during the presidential-election campaign concerned Taiwan's latest and currently biggest 'platform' defence investment: the Tsai

Figure 3: **People's Liberation Army (PLA) incursions into Taiwan's Air Defence Identification Zone (ADIZ), January 2022–December 2023**

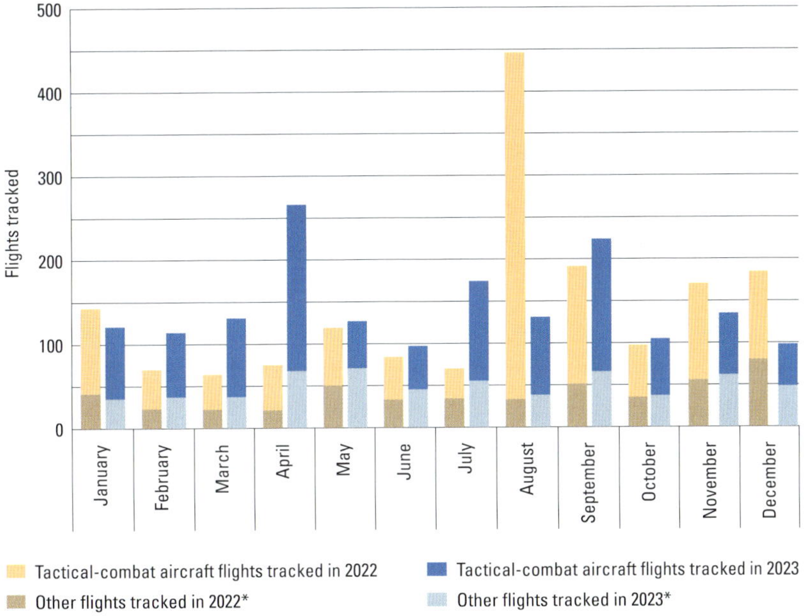

- Tactical-combat aircraft flights tracked in 2022
- Tactical-combat aircraft flights tracked in 2023
- Other flights tracked in 2022*
- Other flights tracked in 2023*

*'Other flights' include flights by bombers, tankers, special-mission aircraft, helicopters and uninhabited aerial vehicles and balloons
Sources: IISS; Taiwan Ministry of National Defense ©IISS

administration's development and construction of what is to be a fleet of eight Taiwanese-made diesel-powered submarines, the first of which, the *Narwhal*, was launched in September 2023.[12] Taiwan is also developing a fleet of light anti-submarine and anti-air warships.[13]

Some critics argue that in a crisis these submarines could be vulnerable to shortfalls in imported components; others assert that the PLA would likely detect and sink the submarines swiftly. By contrast, proponents say that nothing could be more asymmetric than undersea warfare, and that it will be important for the PLA to harbour doubts about its landing crafts' or aircraft carriers' vulnerability to undersea attack. It could also be important for the Americans and others to know that Taiwan is thereby contributing to this undersea asymmetry and thus adding to their own efforts at thwarting China's anti-access/area-denial (A2/AD) strategy.

With President Lai now in office for the next four years, the submarine programme can be expected to continue. A big question, however, is whether a divided Legislative Yuan will permit the DPP government to continue to expand defence spending as rapidly as occurred in the late years of the Tsai administration. The consensus during the election campaign over defence spending between the three presidential candidates argues for optimism on this point, but the realities of parliamentary politics mean that this is not a certainty.

To expand upon and explain that doubt, the debate about defence needs to be placed in a wider context: that of the overall size and character of Taiwan's armed forces. It is not surprising that the Taiwanese military looks tiny in comparison with China's. What is perhaps surprising, or at least noteworthy, is that it looks small in comparison with that of South Korea, a fellow Asian nation that also feels constantly vulnerable to attack.

Unlike Taiwan, South Korea can be said to enjoy the advantage of housing substantial and powerful US forces to aid its defence against North Korea, an advantage that might have tempted successive South Korean governments to underspend on their own forces. But it has not. South Korea's population of 52.0m is more than double Taiwan's 23.4m, yet as recently as 2021 South Korea's annual defence spending was almost treble Taiwan's. Only with recent double-digit annual increases in its defence budget has Taiwan brought itself more in line with South Korea either in proportion to population or in terms of defence spending as a share of GDP.

Moreover, the responses of these two democracies to their very similar demographic pressures has been different: South Korea has maintained conscription for its armed forces lasting

18–21 months; Taiwan in stages during the 2010s reduced its period of compulsory military service to just four months, raising that requirement back to 12 months only in 2022, a measure that came into effect in January 2024 but which (as in South Korea) applies only to men.[14] South Korea's active military force of 500,000 compares with 169,000 for Taiwan, although Taiwan's reserves of 1.7m are roughly equivalent as a share of population to South Korea's of 3.1m.[15]

What this tells us is that until recently successive democratically elected governments in Taiwan have chosen not to maintain or instil an atmosphere of constant readiness and preparation for war, unlike some of their South Korean counterparts, who also live with an unresolved conflict from seven decades ago. That choice has been partly political: a sense that, if war is seen to be imminent, votes might be lost to parties promising reconciliation with China. It also reflects the predicament of an island stuck seemingly permanently in a kind of existential purgatory or limbo: it needs to be able to defend itself against coercion and invasion, and yet the act of making plans to build that defence has sometimes been thought to risk provoking the very coercion that it seeks to deter. It is only now that the prospects of coercion look inescapably real that a full determination to strengthen the island's defences is taking hold, yet even that determination is manifesting itself within a more restricted set of parameters on defence spending and conscription than in South Korea.

Civil resilience

Beyond simply spending more on defence, one big question for the new Lai administration will be how far it chooses to go in instilling an atmosphere of readiness among the public, by organising or facilitating civil-defence training for ordinary civilians and by making weapons available in secure stores around the island for civilian groups to draw upon during a crisis. A second question is how far it will go in building bigger stocks on the island not just of military necessities but also of the essentials of life, such as food and energy.

Currently, civil-defence training is mainly being supplied by private non-profit groups, of which one of the most prominent is Kuma Academy, founded by a leading campaigner against disinformation, Puma Shen. Dr Shen set up Kuma (which means 'bear') in 2021 to provide training in self-defence, first aid and handling intelligence. The following year Kuma received a pledge of NT$600m (US$19.4m) in funding from Robert Tsao, a former semiconductor entrepreneur who has also pledged to help build 1m combat drones to boost the island's defences.[16] Yet the task of civil-defence training is huge: by October 2023, when this author interviewed Dr Shen, just 15,000 people had passed through Kuma's courses against a goal of 2m within the next couple of years. Dr Shen was then elected to the Legislative Yuan as a DPP member in the 2024 elections. He immediately began to campaign for a higher priority to be given to cyber defence, too.[17]

A lot can be achieved – and has been – by such non-profit groups. Some estimates claim that 1.6m Taiwanese people already see themselves as 'preppers' – people who are preparing to resist and survive an invasion – but the Kuma Academy numbers make those estimates look exaggerated.[18] However, a great deal more could be achieved and, even better, demonstrated both to the potential adversary and to allies, if central and local governments were to take on civil-defence training themselves. China will surely be expecting resistance in the event of an invasion, and still more so in the event of a successful takeover of the island, given the protests and dissidence it has seen in Hong Kong. But making that training and preparation of a large swathe of the population for potential conflict a high and sustained government priority could shape those expectations further and help influence the political calculations being made about the costs and benefits. There are, of course, those 1.7m reserves to be called upon in a time of crisis, but with many of the younger ones having spent only four months in conscripted military service there is a strong case for widening training and knowledge a lot further.

Taiwan is already battle-hardened in the fight against disinformation, with official efforts led by the Ministry of Digital Affairs combining well with private efforts led by non-profits such as Dr Shen's Doublethink Lab and others including the Taiwan branch of the Westminster Foundation for Democracy, which is funded by the United Kingdom's Foreign, Commonwealth and Development Office.[19] While the information war is now permanent, Taiwan has been remarkably successful in resisting the waves of Chinese propaganda coming through social media of various forms. That success, combined with Taiwan's high level of technological sophistication, will have been noted in China, for currently the indications are that while such disinformation achieves some tactical gains, it is failing to sway substantial numbers of voters in elections or to make public opinion more favourable in general to China. These efforts at influence and misinformation will no doubt continue, but Taiwan appears well able to cope with them.

The island is less well prepared in terms of the stocks of essentials that would be needed to enable it to survive an invasion or blockade for long enough to allow support to arrive or to convince the adversary to back down. Energy is a particular vulnerability, one that shows up even in peacetime in occasional blackouts. Virtually all the island's energy is imported, with (in 2022) 43.7% of the supply coming from oil, 29.7% from coal, 19.1% from natural gas and just 4.9% and 2.6% from nuclear and renewables respectively.[20] Some of that coal is imported from China, but more than half came from Australia in 2022.[21] The DPP has committed itself to phasing out all nuclear power by 2025. Ambitious plans exist to boost investment in solar and offshore wind power, but they are vulnerable to cross-strait tensions, especially given Chinese firms' dominant position in those industries worldwide.[22] Meanwhile, Taiwan's storage tanks hold only 14 days of supply of liquefied natural gas; the Ministry of Economic Affairs' rule is that oil refiners and importers must keep stocks of at least 60 days of supply while the government itself must keep an oil-security stockpile of at least 30 days.[23] It is a buffer, but not a particularly reassuring one.

This reluctance to spend on energy investment or to build large stockpiles is not the result of any weakness in the Taiwanese economy or in public finances. The Taiwanese government has one of the lowest levels of net public debt in proportion to GDP in the world. Economic growth is not stellar but in recent years has been more than respectable for what is now a mature, wealthy economy.

The strangest aspect of the economy is the extreme undervaluation of the nation's currency, the New Taiwan Dollar, which has contributed to the build-up of a large current-account surplus (12.1% of GDP in 2024, more than eight times as large on that measure as China's).[24] A non-profit lobby group representing US manufacturers, the Coalition for a Prosperous America (CPA), has calculated that in June 2023 the New Taiwan Dollar was nearly 50% undervalued against the US dollar.[25] The cheap currency makes exports – such as semiconductors – cheaper but imports more expensive, while also making the Taiwanese feel poor when they travel overseas. Most of all, though, this economic policy risks building enmity abroad, notably in the US, where the Treasury has not yet labelled Taiwan a 'currency manipulator' and threatened to impose tariffs but could do so under a less friendly future administration.[26]

No Taiwanese government can be in any doubt that the island needs friends, especially the US but also in its own region. Although the number of countries that accord diplomatic recognition to Taiwan is now down to just 11 of the 193 United Nations member states,[27] the island's unofficial relations with other countries in East and Southeast Asia have been strengthening gradually, partly because of the Tsai administration's 'New Southbound Policy' of promoting trade and investment diversification away from China.[28] After China and Hong Kong, which received 35.2% of Taiwan's exports in 2023, according to the Ministry of Finance's Annual External Trade Report the next biggest markets were the Association of Southeast Asian Nations (ASEAN) countries (17.6%), the US (also 17.6%), Europe (9.8%) and Japan (7.3%).[29] The undervalued currency and huge current-account surplus enjoyed by Taiwan, whose own tariffs on imports remain surprisingly high given the country's exporting success, puts those non-Chinese trading partners' sympathy and support for the island at risk, and thereby undermines the credibility of its deterrence.

Narrative clarity

Those economic policies have been consistent now for quite some time and deserve to be changed. But another sort of consistency stands to be even more important, and in this case how it is maintained and explained will be critical. This is the country's narrative about its own status.

The trends of public opinion are, as noted earlier, moving clearly in favour of maintaining the status quo of de facto independence. The election of Lai Ching-te as president means that Taiwanese politics will remain independence-minded for at least the next four years, even though Lai has promised not to make any moves towards a formal change of Taiwan's status. This should permit a helpful clarity in the new government's policies towards defence and civil training, and represents consistency with the previous eight years of the Tsai administration.

From a deterrence point of view, however, such consistency and clarity risk being double-edged. On the one hand, consistency and clarity enhance deterrence by reducing doubt or the possibility of delusion in the adversary's mind about the government's determination to reinforce its defence, to fight disinformation and to ensure that its citizenry is prepared. As Ukraine showed in 2014–22, between the Crimea annexation and the full invasion, preparation takes time and although it can avert defeat it may not be sufficient to deter invasion. On the other hand, such preparations, especially in the hands of a president who formerly spoke up for *de jure* independence, can act as both provocation and justification for Chinese pressure or even invasion. The more determined the island appears to be about maintaining its autonomy, the more it risks helping write China's own narrative about breaching the status quo.

For this reason, the new Lai government would be well advised to combine an increased investment in defence and civil preparation with a stronger communications campaign defining its own intentions. President Lai has entered office with the reputation of being from the 'deep-green', pro-independence side of the DPP, and will thus generate suspicions that he might wish to emulate his DPP presidential predecessor but one, Chen Shui-bian (2000–08), by promoting independence through a referendum or other measures. His comment in July 2023 that his hope was to have a Taiwanese president 'enter the White House' clearly indicated a desire to raise Taiwan's international status.[30] An early gesture to confirm that he now wishes to maintain the status quo could be helpful.

To that end, three distinguished American China scholars, Bonnie Glaser, Jessica Chen Weiss and Thomas J. Christensen, have made the good suggestion that as well as emphasising continuity with the Tsai administration's cross-strait policy, Lai should 'consider revisiting a proposal made by DPP legislators in 2014 to suspend the independence clause in the 1991 party charter, a nonbinding and reversible step that would give any rhetorical commitment to the status quo more weight and credibility'.[31] Such a gesture would go some way towards helping shape the American debate about Taiwan during its own election year, reassuring Taiwan's friends in Southeast Asia and, even more critically, shaping diplomatic and military thinking in China.

CHAPTER SIX

Coercive China, deterrent China

In August 2023 the Chinese state broadcaster, CCTV, released an eight-part documentary series about the People's Liberation Army (PLA) called *Chasing Dreams*, timed, as previous such broadcasts have been, for the anniversary of the PLA's founding in 1927.[1] The opening episode included striking footage and interviews with PLA servicemen about their readiness to invade and conquer Taiwan. Designed to show that the PLA's military exercises directly simulate attacks on Taiwan and that Chinese forces are ready to do so at short notice, the documentary series clearly had a powerful but dual purpose: to reassure domestic Chinese audiences that on the 96th anniversary of its founding, the PLA is well prepared to fulfil the national ambition of reunification; and to send a message of deterrence to Taiwan and to its supporters in the United States to dissuade them from contemplating moves towards independence or any recognition of Taiwan as a sovereign state.

This documentary essentially repeated in a more publicly accessible form the message that had been sent a year earlier, when following the controversial visit to Taiwan by Nancy Pelosi, then speaker of the US House of Representatives, along with a congressional delegation, the PLA conducted a huge military exercise all around the island. Some of the footage in the documentary series came from that demonstrative exercise. As the US Department of Defense (DoD) wrote in its annual report on China to Congress in November 2023, 'the PLA practiced elements of each of its military courses of action against Taiwan during its August 2022 large-scale military exercise aimed at pressuring Taiwan, and again in April 2023 in response to Taiwan president Tsai Ing-wen's transit of the United States'.[2]

On the face of it, therefore, China's deterrence strategy looks simple and consistent, and it blends with its coercion strategy. Deterrence has always been necessary to try to discourage a unilateral declaration of independence by whoever is in government in Taipei. Successive Chinese leaderships have stated openly and plainly that they would respond with force to any move by Taiwan to declare independence, and the only thing that has changed over time is that as the PLA has grown in size and sophistication, so the threatened response has grown more credible, as has been demonstrated in these sorts of exercises.

Meanwhile, however, just as, prior to US President Joe Biden's assertions in 2021–22 that he would be willing to get involved militarily to defend Taiwan if China invaded, the US has practised so-called 'strategic ambiguity' over whether it would intervene, so China has been somewhat ambiguous about what, apart simply from agreeing to reunification and eschewing formal independence, it wants the Taiwanese to do. The Anti-Secession Law passed by China in 2005 was very clear on what Taiwan should not do, but rather less so about what other Taiwanese conduct might be considered unacceptable.[3] That, however, fits in with a general People's Republic of China (PRC) approach of defining unacceptable conduct in retrospect, rather than in advance.

One apparent red line has, seemingly paradoxically, been any move by Taiwan to amend the clauses in the Republic of

China constitution that lay claim to mainland China or any move to relinquish associated claims to territories in the South China Sea: by relinquishing the declared aim of retaking the mainland, Taiwan would be deemed to be formally rejecting the 'One China' principle. Such a red line is tantamount to holding Taiwan in a sort of trap, albeit in a somewhat formulaic and unconvincing way. China, however, has defined the status quo as meaning that the two sides should be moving actively towards reunification. So those aggressive military exercises and the intensification of grey-zone incursions into Taiwanese air and sea space can be seen not just as acts of deterrence but also as efforts to coerce Taiwan into negotiation or to punish it for failing to do so.

Yet this interpretation does not fit well with the fact that it was the PRC's own decision in 2016 to suspend official cross-strait talks when president Tsai took office. Those eight talk-free years are now presumably about to be followed by another four unless China decides to somehow throw down the gauntlet to President Lai Ching-te and seek to compel him to negotiate under threat of conflict. If it were to come about, such a policy would indicate a remarkably high level of confidence that the PLA is now capable of succeeding in the sort of invasion shown in the documentary series and that the US is not in fact likely to risk a third world war by intervening to block it.

For all the bravado of those exercises and the grey-zone intimidation, it does not yet look plausible that China would be prepared to take that risk, at least unless it could convince itself that the US would stand aside.[4] Perhaps, therefore, the real explanation is a simpler one: that following the popular backlash against negotiations during the last Kuomintang presidency, that of Ma Ying-jeou (2008–16), it has become clear to the PRC's leadership that even under a relatively pro-China Taiwanese government progress is difficult, so it is not worth pretending to try during times when the Democratic Progressive Party (DPP) is in power. It is better, on this view, to keep on intimidating Taiwan militarily and diplomatically, and eroding some of its trappings of autonomous status such as its Air Defence Identification Zone, territorial waters and the formerly adhered to median demarcation line in the Taiwan Strait. That way, Taiwan can be made to look and feel less and less viable as an autonomous entity.

The ultimate Chinese goal remains, of course, one of taking over the island and its dependencies. In August 2022, while those intimidatory military exercises were still under way, the Taiwan Affairs Office of the PRC's State Council published its first 'White Paper' on Taiwan for more than two decades so as to reiterate that goal.[5]

The White Paper opened by stating unequivocally that 'resolving the Taiwan question and realizing China's complete reunification … is indispensable for the realization of China's rejuvenation'. It followed its predecessors in 1993 and 2000, and precedent from statements in the late 1970s, in declaring that a policy of 'one country, two systems' would be applied to Taiwan as it was to Hong Kong in 1997, leaving the province a great deal of autonomy if its residents showed that they were 'patriotic'. But the 2022 document used tougher language than its predecessors to instil a sense of urgency about reunification and to accuse both the US and Taiwan's DPP of plotting against it to use Taiwan as a 'pawn' in efforts to 'contain' China.[6]

The White Paper's language about how wonderful reunification would be for the Taiwanese people and how happy they would all be about China's rejuvenation stood in stark contrast to the sense that the PRC has pretty much given up hope of achieving peaceful unification by a straightforward negotiation or process of persuasion. Nor did it recognise in any meaningful way the fact that one country, two systems was largely brought to a halt in Hong Kong in 2020, 27 years ahead of schedule, amongst other things by the passing of a new National Security Law under the provisions of which large numbers of dissidents have been imprisoned. The trajectory of Hong Kong has not, to say the least, acted as a persuasive example for Taiwan.

In terms of the yardsticks for deterrence, this means that while China scores highly on the consistency of its goals and general attitude, it looks rather less good in terms of clarity of approach: the objective may be obvious, but the means and the timeline are not. That may not in the end be unhelpful to China, since keeping the adversary guessing is generally advantageous and is in line with the PRC's mostly ambiguous approach in its foreign policy of avoiding firmly defined propositions lest they encumber it later. However, if we measure the PRC's deterrence strategy against the need to reduce or at least manage the risks of its actions giving rise to a catastrophic conflict, that lack of clarity could end up being harmful.

The best outcome, and one that PRC planners and leaders might therefore be expected to be trying to work towards, would be a takeover which, assuming it must be a coerced one, nonetheless is not challenged militarily by the US and others, and so bears much less risk of escalation.

Put into that more realistic framework of averting the danger of a cataclysmic war, the tasks for a Chinese deterrence strategy, beyond discouraging a declaration of independence, can be examined under three headings:
1. The need to deter the US and its allies from intervening militarily to thwart an invasion or blockade.
2. The need to control the risk of any conflict turning nuclear.
3. The need to control the narrative, to convince as many countries as possible, including the US, that Taiwan is not worth fighting over.

Deterring an intervention

Maps of the Western Pacific used by the US armed forces and by security analysts clearly show what they see as the PRC's main strategy to try to deter outside forces from intervening in a conflict over Taiwan. The large area on such maps labelled as 'anti-access/area denial' (A2/AD), an area that has expanded steadily during the past two decades, represents the area in which Chinese submarines and missiles would now make it perilous for a US-led expeditionary force to enter or to remain present in during a conflict. That A2/AD area now extends well beyond the first island chain around the South China and East China seas and into the Pacific towards Guam. The costs of mounting a counter-intervention, to use the term of art, have been rising steadily.

The question, however, as for all acts of deterrence, is whether those costs have risen to a level high enough to make a counter-intervention unlikely. There are two reasons to think that they have not, which arise from weaknesses in this deterrence strategy.

The first is that if US or allied forces choose to enter or remain in this A2/AD area, it places the burden of escalation onto China. That is why gaming simulations of how an attempted invasion of Taiwan would play out generally assume that an invasion would have to commence with synchronised missile attacks both on Taiwanese air and sea defences and on US and Japanese bases in Okinawa, the main Japanese islands and Guam, and potentially South Korea.[7] In other words, if this assumption turns out to be accurate, it means that A2/AD would not be considered secure and reliable enough for the PLA to simply leave such attacks as an implicit threat; the 'denial' would have to be implemented upfront. The option that Chinese propaganda appears to define as preferable – namely that a conflict or confrontation with Taiwan would be characterised as simply being an internal matter between the PRC and its renegade province that others should stand aside from – would thereby be made unavailable. The threat of those missile attacks is a threat of pre-emption, and thereby of the declaration of war, not of deterrence.

The alternative, surely preferred, scenario would be for China to have assured itself in advance that America would not attempt to intervene. Certainly, the perceived potency of the PLA's missiles, bombers and submarines could play a part in such a decision, so it is true that A2/AD can thereby be seen to have deterrent value. But this depends on a US president taking the same view of Taiwan as Biden did of Ukraine – that it was not worth risking the start of a third world war over by challenging those A2/AD perimeters. Absent an assurance of this in advance, the decision over whether to risk a third world war would, initially at least, be a Chinese one.

The second weakness reinforces the first. Unless China has already declared war on the US by the time of (or immediately before) making pre-emptive strikes, an equally likely scenario is that the US president would inform his or her Chinese counterpart that unless the attack on Taiwan is called off by a certain deadline, US forces will intervene. Chinese missile attacks on Taiwanese defences might not provide the time for such communication to happen, but an associated amphibious landing would do so, as there are 160 kilometres of sea to be crossed. In any event, as with Russia's invasion of Ukraine, American intelligence would almost certainly have detected preparations for a seaborne invasion well in advance. A surprise missile attack could be possible, but a surprise seaborne attack would not.

The advantage of geography does mean that it would take time for the US armed forces to arrive at scale. But if an American president were prepared to intervene, US forces would be able to do so in still-damaging ways much sooner, chiefly by using submarines and uninhabited undersea vessels but also airpower and long-range missiles as well, potentially, as cyber and space-based systems. Moreover, stealth technology, precision guidance and drones have all improved even as China's A2/AD capabilities have been built up.

A threat to intervene unless the attack were called off would therefore carry potency, which is why it is reasonable to believe that an American president with the opportunity to make such a threat would do so. China's A2/AD capabilities are highly significant, but they are by no means impregnable.[8] Both sides would still have the chance, and the incentive, to call each other's bluff. The two sides' deterrence strategies would, in effect, be standing nose to nose, with the key question, likely unanswerable in advance in a convincing way, being whether either side was willing to threaten or even use nuclear weapons.

The fundamental issue for both the US and China therefore remains one of whether their leaderships were willing to risk, and then likely fight, an all-out conflict between the world's two most powerful military forces, and therefore revolves around their respective judgements about the relative strengths of those forces and of those of allies that would be willing to join each of them. While China typically characterises the US strategy of integrated deterrence as 'containment', there is little clear evidence of how PRC decision-makers assess its strengths and weaknesses nor of its impact on their own calculations.

Controlling the nuclear risk

Recent editions of the Pentagon's 'China Military Power Report' (its annual report to Congress on 'Military and Security Developments Involving the People's Republic of China') have highlighted the fact that China is currently undertaking a substantial expansion of its arsenal of nuclear weapons.[9] The 2023 report stated that the DoD believes that by May 2023, the PRC's arsenal had expanded to more than 500 operational nuclear warheads (from 'the low 200s', according to the DoD's 2020 report) and that by 2030 the number of operational warheads would likely have risen to over 1,000.[10] As China does not report on the status of its nuclear forces and nor is there in place a process of disclosure and verification between the US and China, these numbers remain estimates. But successive Pentagon reports have backed such estimates up with evidence of large new silo fields spread across various locations around China. The DoD has also reported that Russia is supplying enriched uranium for China's fast-breeder nuclear reactors, which implies that this is being used to produce the plutonium required for this nuclear-weapons expansion.[11]

Ever since it became a nuclear-weapons state, China's nuclear policy has been described as one of 'minimal deterrence'. This means that rather than holding a stock of nuclear weapons sufficient to make an adversary share a mutual sense of vulnerability to a nuclear cataclysm, as summarised by the term 'mutually assured destruction', the Chinese arsenal was considered adequate to convince any adversary that they would be likely to suffer highly damaging retaliation in the event of a nuclear attack. The definition of 'adequate' under this notion means sufficient nuclear capacity to survive an opponent's first strike and guarantee that they would be hit by a second strike, and thus to create the expectation that they would be deterred by that prospect alone. The question now, as China has more than doubled its stock of nuclear warheads over the past decade and is set to double the stock again by the end of the 2020s, is what this means for the PRC's nuclear doctrine. As Fiona Cunningham wrote in an authoritative analysis for the Arms Control Association in June 2023, 'policymakers and scholars outside of China do not know why Beijing is rapidly modernizing its nuclear arsenal'.[12]

As Figure 4 shows, even at 1,000 warheads in 2030, China will have a far smaller arsenal than either the US or Russia. The ultimate objective, nonetheless, may well be one of nuclear equivalence, perhaps by the time of the oft-cited 100th anniversary of the People's Republic in 2049, an objective that would fit in with the general aim, defined by President Xi Jinping, of having a 'world-class' military by then. Meanwhile, though, the important issue is what, if anything, this nuclear build-up means for Taiwan during the intervening decades and, more particularly, for the ability or willingness of the US and its allies to intervene militarily in the event of a Chinese invasion or other form of coercion.

Since we cannot know the definitive answer to this, the appropriate response has to be one of cautious preparedness.

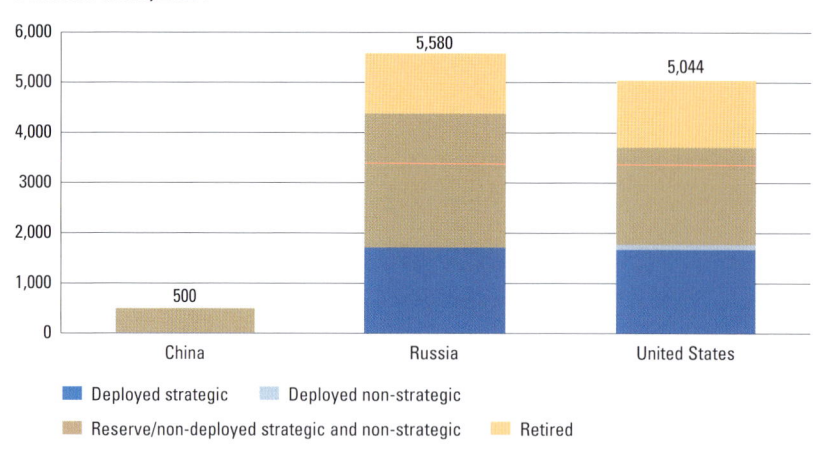

Figure 4: **Estimated nuclear-warhead inventories of China, Russia and the United States, 2024**

China	500
Russia	5,580
United States	5,044

Legend: Deployed strategic | Deployed non-strategic | Reserve/non-deployed strategic and non-strategic | Retired

Notes from source: Total inventory includes stockpiled and retired warheads; stockpiled warheads include deployed and reserve warheads; deployed warheads include those on ballistic missiles, at bomber bases and, in the case of the US, non-strategic bombs in Europe. The Chinese stockpile is increasing, and in 2022 the US Department of Defense claimed that by 2030 China's nuclear stockpile 'will have about 1,000 operational nuclear warheads'. Part of that increase is already well under way and our estimate includes some of it; however, these claims depend on many uncertain factors, including how many missile silos will be built, how many warheads each missile will carry, and assumptions about the future production of fissile materials by China. China considers all of its nuclear weapons to be strategic, but the US military calls its medium- and intermediate-range missile non-strategic.

Source: Adapted from Hans M. Kristensen, Matt Korda, Eliana Johns, and Mackenzie Knight, Federation of American Scientists, 2024

Note: The IISS assesses that some of China's warheads are actively deployed aboard its SSBNs, which the US DoD believes conduct near-continuous at-sea deterrence patrols. However, it is unknown precisely how many boats are on patrol at any one time and whether they are equipped with the single-warhead JL-2 or MIRVed JL-3.   ©IISS

Accordingly, Brandon J. Babin, a senior analyst for the US Indo-Pacific Command, takes a pessimistic view in a new book on China's approach to deterrence.[13] Babin argues that what China has been developing is a 'graduated nuclear deterrent', a strategy which for the first time has incorporated plans for lower-yield warheads (often known as 'tactical nuclear weapons' or 'non-strategic nuclear weapons') and which reflects a change of view about the utility of nuclear war.[14] He cites the PLA's 2012 *Encyclopedia of China's Strategic Missile Force* as stating that there was no longer unanimity that nuclear war was uncontrollable and that 'limited nuclear war had limited risk' because such tactical weapons could be used to warn and deter an opponent.[15] At the same time, China has been developing (and displaying) an increasingly powerful 'nuclear triad' of land-based intercontinental ballistic missiles (ICBMs), submarine-launched ballistic missiles and strategic bombers.

Babin argues that well before the long-term benefits of strategic equivalence to the US might be reached, China's view may be that by having a credible and graduated nuclear deterrent it can gain the leverage it needs to force Taiwan back to the negotiating table because only such a deterrent will stand a chance of persuading America not to intervene militarily on the island's side. On this view, China must show that it has options both of countering the use of tactical nuclear weapons and of striking the US homeland. The combined deterrent and compellent would therefore not be area denial but nuclear denial.

Other important issues arise from China's nuclear-modernisation and build-up programme, including notably the lack of clarity about whether missile silos and other elements of the triad contain conventional or nuclear warheads, raising the prospect of a conventional conflict turning nuclear inadvertently. But those issues are beyond the purview of this book, which is how any large-scale war, whether conventional or nuclear, can be deterred and avoided, and how countries' strategies measure up against that task. For those questions, what matters is what effect China's nuclear build-up could have on the psychology of political and military leaders in Washington, Taipei and allied capitals such as Tokyo.

This really depends on two factors, which will necessarily remain uncertain and probably variable according to circumstance: firstly, the willingness (and, critically, the perceived willingness) of Chinese political and military leaders to use nuclear weapons of any kind in a conflict with the US; and secondly, the priority US leaders assign at any given time to protecting Taiwan and to preventing China from achieving military control over the South China and East China seas.

Currently, the prime evidence about that willingness is President Xi's public reaction in November 2022 to the threats by his strategic partner, President Vladimir Putin, of using nuclear weapons in Russia's war on Ukraine. The world, Xi said, should 'advocate that nuclear weapons cannot be used, a nuclear war cannot be waged'.[16] It is naturally reasonable to doubt whether Xi or a successor would maintain this view during an actual or potential conflict in which China itself was involved. The same can be said of the PRC's long-declared 'no first use' policy: we cannot know how well this would hold up under the pressure of real conflict. But in any case, if China's more capable and resilient nuclear forces were to be used as a deterrent, the messaging would have to change.

Controlling the narrative

In the short or medium term, messaging aimed at influencing thinking about whether Taiwan and the first island chain really matter looks to be a more useful tool for China to use than the nuclear threat. However, even on this point, China's starting point is not a good one.

If China were to base its thinking about the prospects of an invasion or coercion of Taiwan leading to a US intervention and full-scale war on the reported private comments by then-president Donald Trump in 2019 to an unnamed US senator, it might think itself safe to do whatever it pleases as soon as the White House is again occupied either by him or by someone who thinks like him. To remind the reader, the *Washington Post* columnist Josh Rogin quoted Trump as having said 'Taiwan is like two feet from China. We are eight thousand miles away. If they invade there isn't a fucking thing we can do about it.'[17]

However, China knows very well that this is not how the Pentagon would brief a US president if a crisis were to be emerging, and nor can the PRC have been sure that Trump actually meant or understood what he is reported to have said. The Pentagon's briefing would say that US forces much closer than 8,000 miles away can do a lot about an invasion. Moreover, even if a president did share the view that Trump reportedly held, it would be a view that goes against all the rest of what has become the prevailing bipartisan narrative in Washington DC: that China is America's 'pacing competitor'; that it must be confronted on economic, technological and geopolitical grounds; that its defence build-up needs to be countered; and that it would be disastrous for America's strategic position in the Pacific if China were to hold Taiwan and to be able to treat the South China and East China seas as 'a Chinese lake'.[18]

Moreover, Trump's reported statement of US impotence also goes against the diplomatic trend of his own administration: before his 2017 inauguration he breached previous conventions by taking a congratulatory call from president Tsai – the first time US and Taiwanese leaders had spoken directly to one another for 40 years – and during his administration contacts were stepped up between senior officials of the US and Taiwan.[19] Furthermore, both Trump and President Biden have authorised large packages of arms sales to Taiwan, including in Biden's case one that included for the first time a grant under the Foreign Military Financing scheme, a programme previously used only for sovereign states.[20] There is more bipartisan support in the US Congress for arms sales to Taiwan than there is for Ukraine.

From China's point of view, this means that it is failing to control the narrative surrounding Taiwan. In American political circles that narrative has drifted towards treating Taiwan as if it were independent. China's own position is perfectly clear. However, in order to make the desired reunification easier and to deter the US and others from intervening to defend Taiwan, a further narrative message would be needed: that while Taiwan is important to us, for historical and cultural reasons, it is not important enough to you to expend blood and treasure on.

This requires China to downplay all notions that Taiwan's location makes it strategically important, and ideally to support that message by showing that the PRC, too, supports full freedom of navigation in the surrounding seas and has no intention of making those seas a Chinese lake. That would, however, be in contradiction with China's current daily actions in those seas, with its refusal to accept international judicial rulings concerning territory in those seas, and with its failure to reach agreement with the other littoral nations on a maritime code of conduct, which has been under discussion for nearly three decades.[21]

Speeches by the Chinese minister of defence at the IISS Shangri-La Dialogue each June in Singapore routinely assert that US ships and planes have no business operating in the South China and East China seas, and that their presence there is some sort of impingement on Chinese sovereignty. This leaves audiences to guess as to who China thinks does have the right to operate in those international waters if the Americans do not.

In fact, at present China is forcing the narrative in the opposite direction from the one that would best suit its own interests concerning Taiwan: it is making the future status of that small island look more important rather than less. For a whole variety of reasons – political, economic and technological – it certainly looks more important now to Australia, Japan and the Philippines, which are the most critical allies for the US and Taiwan in the region, but also to a range of others.

CHAPTER SEVEN

Allies and partners: the role of Japan

Apart from the United States itself, no Western-aligned country is more important in terms of deterring war over Taiwan than Japan, and no country has a greater interest in contributing to that deterrence, as best it can. But also, no country in the Indo-Pacific, with the possible exception of South Korea, has a greater need to ensure, over the coming decades, that it will still be able to defend itself and its interests if the US were to become not just the sometimes unpredictable ally that it already is but also one that decides to disengage itself from the region. Building self-reliance cannot be done quickly: Japan has, of course, been highly dependent on its security alliance with the US ever since the US occupation ended in 1951, and in fact the security treaty was partly designed to make Japan dependent as well as useful. But this task is not one just for the next five years but rather for the next 50 years, and beyond. The good news is that the work has begun. The difficult question to answer is that of how vulnerable Japan will be at different points in the 2030s, 2040s and 2050s during that process of building greater self-reliance and hedging against America's future evolution.

For the time being, however, we can focus on how Japan will contribute to US strategy in the Indo-Pacific while also addressing what the limitations currently are to that contribution and how much Japan can do on its own. As was noted in earlier chapters, America's strategy of 'integrated deterrence' combines a message of deterrent activity and capabilities being coordinated across multiple domains, with one of activity and capabilities being coordinated with multiple international allies and partners.[1] Since the Biden administration entered office in 2021, that coordination with allies and partners has made notable progress: the AUKUS deal was struck in 2021 between Australia, the United Kingdom and the US to share advanced technology, particularly for a new Australian fleet of nuclear-propelled submarines that will patrol the Pacific in the 2040s; talks in the Quadrilateral Security Dialogue (the Quad) between Australia, India, Japan and the US have become institutionalised; under the two countries' Enhanced Defense Cooperation Agreement the Philippines has agreed to provide and improve logistics facilities for US use at more bases, now a total of nine,[2] on four islands of the Philippine archipelago; and above all, Japan has announced plans for a dramatic, and potentially transformational, increase in its defence spending and hence in its military, intelligence, communications and cyber capabilities over the next five years. These plans were extended during a state visit to the US in April 2024 by Prime Minister Kishida Fumio to include discussions about instituting mechanisms for joint command and control of Japanese and US forces, a topic that had previously been taboo.[3]

It has all been a big diplomatic success, to which can be added another American achievement: helping to persuade two of its closest Indo-Pacific allies, Japan and South Korea, to resume summitry and military and intelligence collaboration with each other, after several years during which tensions over the legacy of Japan's colonisation of Korea (1910–45) had put such collaboration into the deep freeze.[4] This in part also reflects South Korea's decision to expand its official security thinking beyond the Korean Peninsula and towards the wider region, publishing its first formal Indo-Pacific strategy in 2022.[5]

This diplomatic success is important: it reconfirms the fact that America's network of allies and partners is much larger and more deeply connected than China's, even in China's backyard, and that the network is not just theoretical but in practical ways is working to improve national and regional security. Meanwhile, America's NATO allies in further-flung Europe have been lining up to publish Indo-Pacific strategies of their own, as well as sailing naval ships into the region and, in France's case, flying in fighter squadrons.

Yet the question must be asked: what difference will all this make to deterrence? It is undoubtedly helpful. But how helpful? To answer that requires us to apply some of the yardsticks from Chapter Three, first to Japan and then, in Chapter Eight, to other allies and partners:

1. Political will: is this integration of Japanese forces likely to be maintained through electoral cycles and evolving circumstances?
2. Military capability: would the US and China expect the capabilities provided by Japan to be available quickly enough and in sufficient quantity to make a difference in the case of an invasion?
3. Narrative: do the narratives used by Japan support the broader goal of preventing a full-scale war and promoting the region's prosperity, and do they convey an agreed position on what is meant by the status quo?

Japan, from self-defence to constrained deterrence

The most significant of these developments among America's allies and partners is the defence transformation taking place in Japan. It is significant firstly because of its scale: the measures set in train by the current Liberal Democratic Party (LDP) government, under Prime Minister Kishida, will, if fully implemented, give Japan what is likely to rank by 2027 among the world's five biggest defence budgets, climbing from ninth place in 2023.[6] Under a new National Security Strategy, National Defense Strategy and Defense Buildup Program, all released in December 2022, Japan has said it intends to raise its annual spending to the NATO target level of 2% of GDP by 2027, which will mean an estimated increase of 60% over five years.[7] In association with that increase, the government intends to give a major boost to its domestic defence industry, the most eye-catching part of which is a joint project with the UK and Italy to develop and build a next-generation fighter jet to be delivered in 2035.[8] But it is also significant for reasons of geography: the Japanese archipelago represents a vast 'island chain' in its own right, stretching more than 3,000 kilometres from the Sea of Okhotsk in the north, bordering Russia, all the way down to the island of Yonaguni, between the Philippine Sea and the East China Sea, just 100 km from Taiwan.

Finally, the Japanese defence transformation is significant for what it symbolises: the return of Japan – the region's earliest and most successful moderniser but also its defeated twentieth-century coloniser – as a military power rather than solely being what a long-serving prime minister of the 1980s, Nakasone Yasuhiro, termed 'an unsinkable aircraft-carrier' for the US – though it still plays that role, given the major US bases on the island of Okinawa as well as on three of Japan's four main islands.[9]

Not that Japan entirely went away: although its armed forces have since 1954 been named the Japan Self-Defense Forces (JSDF), they are already large and potent by world standards, even if not by those of either the US or China. As befits the archipelago's geographical scope, its Maritime Self-Defense Force (JMSDF) is especially noteworthy, with 52 principal surface combatants (the category used in the IISS *Military Balance*), more than double the number of principal surface combatants in either the French or British navies. The JMSDF includes four aircraft carriers: initially deployed as helicopter carriers, the two largest are soon to be converted to carry F-35B combat aircraft.[10] Japan also has a large and well-armed coastguard fleet, spending on which falls outside the main defence budget.

Yet as things stand, the expanded and strengthened JSDF will still be a military power operating under tight constraints. It was revealing that in his foreword to the Defense White Paper for 2023, Japan's then-minister of defense, Hamada Yasukazu, summed up the reason for this dramatic expansion as follows: 'It is essential to make efforts to "defend our country by ourselves" and increase deterrence. In other words, we need to make the opponent think that "attacking Japan will not achieve its goals".'[11]

Those objectives imply that Japan wishes to reduce its dependence on the US for its own defence and to be able to deter direct attacks on Japanese territory. Both aims are admirable but limited. During a conflict, this stronger JSDF would take some of the burden off US forces based in Japan, while in advance of any conflict they would also help in the deterrence of attacks on Japanese and US bases there. But it is worth noting what these carefully chosen words do not include: participation in a US military intervention to defend Taiwan, or any other third country. This is deterrence of attacks on Japan, not on Taiwan or in the region.

This leads to some contradictory scores about political will and consistency and clarity of deterrence messages, the opening yardstick from Chapter Three. The first, and positive, score is that Japan can be expected to stick to this new defence strategy because the political party that has advocated it, the LDP, looks unchallenged in electoral terms. It has governed Japan since 1955, barring a brief period in 1993 and then three troubled years in 2009–12 when an opposition party, the Democratic Party of Japan, run partly by LDP defectors, gained power but then crumbled. LDP leaders will come and go, brought down often by party-financing and other scandals, but unless the party suffers an electoral defeat, which currently looks hard to imagine given the weakness of all opposition parties, the defence policy will almost certainly be maintained, and will likely continue to be ambitious after 2027.

Since 2012, the LDP has governed in a coalition with Komeito, a centrist Buddhist party, even though it has had sufficient parliamentary strength to govern on its own. The LDP's then-leader, Abe Shinzo, who is the true architect of Japan's defence transformation, wanted the support in electoral organisation and mobilisation that Komeito and its associated Buddhist sect, Soka Gakkai, can provide in addition to giving him a big buffer in terms of parliamentary seats. Komeito's own electoral support is now weakening, giving rise to speculation that the LDP might soon drop it in favour of a rising right-wing party, Nippon Ishin no Kai, known in English as the Japan Innovation Party.

Such a switch, if it happens, could bolster Japan's defence transformation, as the paradox of prime minister Abe's coalition deal with Komeito was that this great foreign-policy hawk was thereby shoring up his political position by linking his party to a group that, officially at least, is pacifist. That paradox continues to pose problems. During 2023, Komeito at first obstructed a reform to Japan's defence-export guidelines that aimed to make it possible for the country to sell enough of the fighter jets it is developing jointly with the UK and Italy to make the project economically viable.[12] Previously, agreement had been reached on permitting exports of Japan-made *Patriot* surface-to-air missiles (SAMs) to the country from which the manufacturing is licensed, the US, which will help refill America's stocks and allow it to export its own *Patriot*s to Ukraine, Taiwan and Israel, among others; and then eventually Komeito gave way on the fighter jets too in March 2024.[13]

If Nippon Ishin no Kai were to replace Komeito at or after the next general election, and if that party's rise continues, political support for defence spending and for easier export laws can be expected to rise.[14] Furthermore, if a political change were to occur in the US that cast doubt on the reliability of the US alliance or on the closeness of the US–Japan relationship, that would simply reinforce the case for this defence strategy in order gradually to reduce Japan's dependence on America. Japan's political will can be counted on to remain strong.

The second, and negative, score on the consistency yardstick is, however, that another sort of consistency should also be expected to prevail: the tight constraints the Japanese constitution sets on military activity. And those constraints mean that a sort of half-joke in security circles has it that whenever war games are run involving several Indo-Pacific allies, the Japanese team has to spend much of its time trying to work out whether particular actions would be permitted by the law.

Article 9 of the Constitution of Japan that was drafted by the Supreme Commander for the Allied Powers during the American occupation, and which came into effect in May 1947, could not have been clearer:

> Aspiring sincerely to an international peace based on justice and order, the Japanese people forever

renounce war as a sovereign right of the nation and the threat or use of force as means of settling international disputes.

In order to accomplish the aim of the preceding paragraph, land, sea, and air forces, as well as other war potential, will never be maintained. The right of belligerency of the state will not be recognized.[15]

Article 96 of the constitution is equally clear about the procedure required for an amendment: a two-thirds majority in both houses of the Diet, and then a simple majority of votes cast in 'a special referendum or at such election as the Diet shall specify'.[16]

In the so-far seven decades of this constitution there have been no revisions nor yet any serious prospect of any proposed revisions facing a national vote. During Abe's premiership, in 2015 he managed to adjust cabinet rules to allow Japan in principle to send its armed forces to support an ally if such 'collective self-defence' could be said to assist Japan's own defence, but that is as far as revision has gone – and even that drew unusually large street protests.[17] Japan does send military forces overseas for peacekeeping operations, but so far always for non-combat roles.[18]

In recent years the LDP–Komeito coalition has frequently commanded a two-thirds majority in both houses. However, the LDP has not formally proposed a revision to Article 9 as the pacifist Komeito has opposed it. If Nippon Ishin no Kai were to replace Komeito, that problem might disappear. But that still leaves the referendum hurdle, which those 2015 protests showed to be a high one. The Ukraine war has boosted public support for the LDP's defence policy but has not made a constitutional referendum look readily winnable: opinion polls in May 2023 for the centre-left *Asahi Shimbun* newspaper and the centre-right *Yomiuri Shimbun* indicated that while a majority might exist for some sort of constitutional change, the country is evenly split on whether Article 9 should be amended.[19] In the *Asahi* poll, 55% of respondents said Article 9 should not be changed, while the *Yomiuri* poll had 51% in favour of amending at least the second paragraph – the one about not maintaining military forces – presumably on grounds that it long ago became a fiction. In principle, Article 96 would allow an LDP-led government to obtain Diet approval for a special election on the issue of Article 9 rather than a referendum, but it would take a bold government to thereby bet all its parliamentary power on this one cause.

These constraints, for as long as they last, must necessarily raise doubts about how Japan could and would react to an attempted Chinese invasion or blockade of Taiwan. If there were to be a direct attack on Japanese territory, whether by China, North Korea or Russia, it is clear that Japan could and would respond. A blockade of Taiwan would be more complicated, as naturally would be an invasion: does Japanese protection of sea lanes constitute self-defence? Would the dispatch of US forces to intervene to defend Taiwan mean that Japanese forces could support them under the principle of collective self-defence?

The answer to both is: probably, but we cannot be sure. In the event of a regional and therefore potentially global crisis, a future LDP prime minister might well feel both emboldened and obliged by the sense of emergency, an emergency that would inevitably put the Japanese archipelago at risk. His or her judgement would no doubt depend on whether they thought the sense of emergency would be enough to quieten the potential public outcry about whether such a move would be illegal.

What is certain is that unless and until Article 9 has been revised, no Japanese prime minister is likely in peacetime to make an unequivocal public declaration of support for the US and Taiwan, even though several ministers have in recent years underlined the importance to Japan of maintaining peace in the Taiwan Strait.[20] This must inevitably reduce the deterrent value of Japan's defence build-up regarding Taiwan, though we cannot know by how much. Chinese decision-makers would surely expect Japan to join an American fight in most circumstances, unless the US–Japan relationship had broken down, but if that were the case then a lot of other things would change too, including probably a new push in Japan both for even stronger defence and for constitutional revision. Chinese decision-makers might tell themselves that the JSDF have had no combat experience since 1945. But then much the same is true of the People's Liberation Army, which last fought in 1979.

Constrained but speedy?

Where Japan's deterrent value is clearer is regarding its two other close and hostile neighbours: North Korea and Russia. The main deterrence for North Korea will remain the US, especially thanks to its extended nuclear deterrence but also its forces on the Korean Peninsula, and a Russian attack would anyway not be considered likely except in the context of a global conflict. But a key element of Japan's defence build-up plan will provide strong support for the conventional deterrence of North Korea: its decision to acquire 'counterstrike capabilities' most immediately in the form of 400 *Tomahawk* land-attack cruise missiles (LACMs) to be bought from the US and installed on JMSDF vessels.[21] Half are expected to arrive during 2025 and the remainder during the following two years. The *Tomahawk*s send a message that any attack on Japan by North Korea, Russia or indeed China can and will be responded to forcefully. There has been some debate about whether such missiles could even be used pre-emptively if convincing evidence of an imminent attack were to be obtained, but so far without any clear conclusion.

Regarding China, that counterstrike capability would really come into play only if the People's Republic of China (PRC) were considering a pre-emptive attack on US and Japanese military assets in Japan and Japanese waters. If the PRC were to be weighing up such an attack, knowledge of the Japanese *Tomahawk*s would likely be of some, albeit marginal importance, given that such an attack would be in effect a declaration of war against both countries. It would affect the targeting more than the decision itself.

The parts of Japan's defence build-up plan that might have most caught the eye of Chinese military planners for the medium term are the intended changes in Japan's communications, intelligence and cyber capabilities, and in the JSDF's force posture. These are less affected by constitutional constraints but are not entirely free of them.

On intelligence and cyber, Japan is building from a low base, but the declared intention is to create, for the first time since 1945, a full external intelligence agency to add human intelligence (HUMINT) to the country's existing (and strong) signals-intelligence capability; and to expand the national cyber-defence force from roughly 500 people now to 20,000.

Both of those efforts will be steep uphill struggles, especially if they are to be anything close to completed within the five years of the current Defense Buildup Program: intelligence, because currently Japan has too many agencies that share too little information between them, and because HUMINT takes years to develop; and cyber, because recruiting and training roughly 5,000 hackers and 15,000 engineers in an already highly competitive labour market will be tough. And there is a legal constraint: hacking is illegal under Japan's 1999 Unauthorised

Computer Access Law, and Article 21 of the constitution protects 'the secrecy of any means of communication', both of which make offensive cyber operations difficult, to say the least.[22]

Nonetheless, however steep the struggles may prove, a big Japanese effort to strengthen the security of communications infrastructure, to invest in intelligence collection and analysis, and to boost cyber defence will help build not only Japan's own resilience but also the combined resilience of all the allies in the region, from the US to Taiwan to South Korea and to the Philippines, thanks to the sharing of intelligence and expertise. And intelligence is an important asset in building relations with other countries, such as Vietnam.

Those contributions can become significant as they develop, but it is the contribution of a changed Japanese force posture that promises to serve deterrence most directly. The reason is geography: Yonaguni, the most southwestern inhabited island in the Japanese archipelago, is only just over 100 km away from Taiwan.

In the past, these Nansei or Ryukyu Islands running southwest from Okinawa have been largely left alone by the JSDF, barring a minimal presence mainly for potential disaster-relief purposes, some porting facilities for the coastguard fleet and some radar sites.[23] Since 2016, however, Japan has been building up on its southwestern islands a range of military facilities and units, including anti-ship missiles, SAMs, electronic warfare and air (see Map 4).[24]

The local politics of doing this are delicate. These islands are mainly accustomed to tourism and fishing. Some islanders perceive the installation of missile-defence units and the arrival of more soldiers as making their homes less secure, not more, as fear grows that this will make the islands a target. But the islands' location so close to a potential war zone means that if a conflict were to break out, they would be affected in any case, making the argument for deterring such a conflict strong. It is perhaps fortunate that fishermen and other sailors on the islands are already well aware of the regular and sizeable incursions into the territorial waters of Japan's Senkaku islands, only 150 km north of Yonaguni, by Chinese fishing boats, coastguards, naval ships and even submarines, as China has stepped up intimidation so as to press its claim on those islands, which it calls the Diaoyu Dao.[25] And they are becoming more aware of US and Japanese naval vessels too, as the two forces have been holding more joint exercises around Yonaguni.

Those exercises carry with them an implication that in due course, or in a crisis, US forces might even be given permission to use Yonaguni and its logistical facilities. Stocks of ammunition, fuel and other supplies are being built up in the islands. The more that the JSDF's force posture is moved closer to Taiwan, and the more that such joint use becomes possible, the more positive will be Japan's contribution to deterrence.

Many unanswered questions

The transformation in Japan's grand strategy was begun in earnest by prime minister Abe during his main period in office in 2012–20 but was really accelerated only with the three new national-security and defence documents of late 2022.[26] While aircraft carriers had been built before then and preparations begun for bases in the Nansei Islands, many of the reforms to Japan's defence practices, organisation and capabilities are either brand new or are yet to happen.

A prime example is that until now the separate services of the JSDF have not had a permanent joint headquarters. The new security strategy set a goal of establishing such a joint command within five years (i.e., by the end of 2027), although it looks likely to be achieved much sooner than that. The previous system depended on allocating joint command to one of the services

128 | Deterrence, Diplomacy and the Risk of Conflict Over Taiwan

Map 4: **Selected changes to Japan's force posture in Kyushu and the southwestern region since 2016**

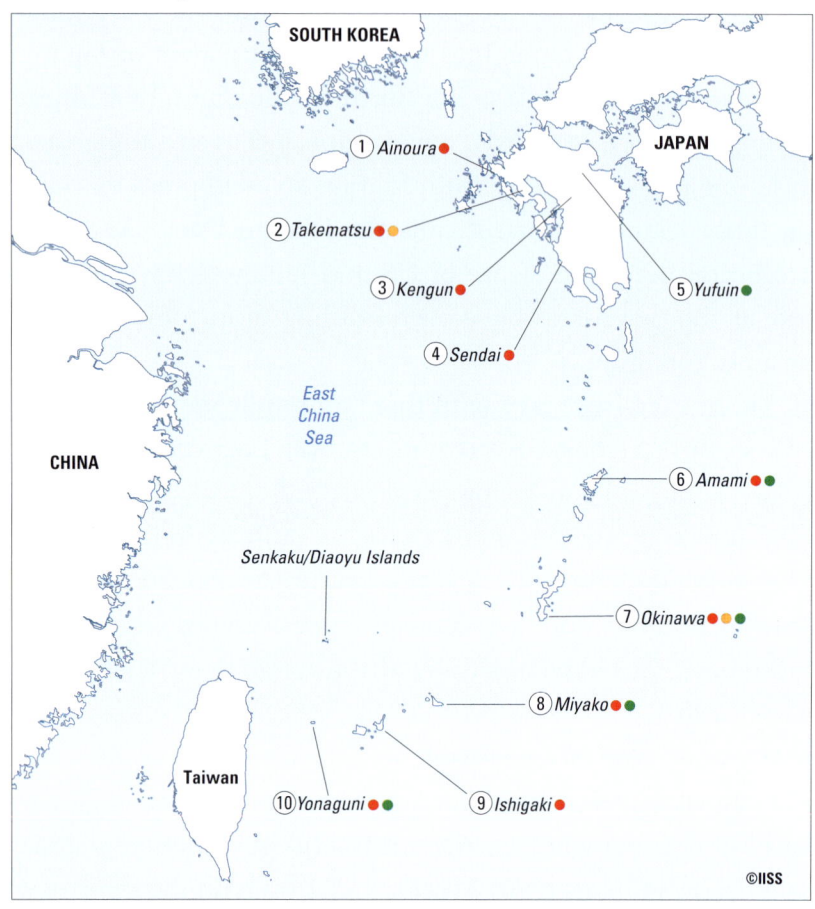

Location	● Established between 2016 and April 2023	● Established April 2023–April 2024	● Planned
① Ainoura	2018 JGSDF Amphibious Rapid Deployment Brigade		
	2022 JGSDF EW unit		
② Takematsu	2022 JGSDF SAM unit	2024 JGSDF 3rd Amphibious Rapid Deployment Regiment	
③ Kengun	2021 JGSDF EW unit		
	2022 JGSDF AShM unit		
④ Sendai	2023 JGSDF EW unit		
⑤ Yufuin			JGSDF AShM unit
⑥ Amami	2019 JGSDF Amami area security unit		Ammunition storage facility
	2019 JGSDF SAM unit		
	2019 JGSDF AShM unit		
	2022 JGSDF EW unit		

⑦ Okinawa	2016 JASDF Air Wing	2024 JGSDF AShM unit	Reorganisation of JGSDF 15th Bde into division-sized unit
	2017 JASDF Southwestern Air Defense Force		
	2017 Southwestern Aircraft Control and Warning Wing		
	2022 JGSDF EW unit		
⑧ Miyako	2019 JGSDF Miyako area security unit		JGSDF EW unit
	2020 JGSDF AShM unit		
	2020 JGSDF SAM unit (redeployed)		
⑨ Ishigaki	2023 JGSDF Yaeyama area security unit		
	2023 JGSDF AShM unit		
	2023 JGSDF SAM unit		
⑩ Yonaguni	2016 JGSDF Yonaguni Coast Observation unit		JGSDF EW unit
	2022 JASDF Warning Squadron (part deployed)		JGSDF SAM unit

Key: AShM: anti-ship missile, EW: electronic warfare, SAM: surface-to-air missile, JGSDF: Japan Ground Self-Defense Force, JASDF: Japan Air Self-Defense Force
Note: Precise unit sizes are unclear.
Sources: Defense of Japan 2023; Japan Ministry of Defense

according to the nature of the contingency – which up until now has usually been a natural disaster or other humanitarian-relief contingency – but that means there is a lack of consistency.

Intelligence also lacks central control or coordination; given Japan's post-war history and internal focus, it is currently dominated by the National Police Agency rather than by an entity in or adjunct to the Ministry of Foreign Affairs or the Cabinet Office, as is normal in other countries. Another example is the lack of a fully fledged security-clearance system, needed to reassure governmental or industrial partners that technological or intelligence secrets can be expected to be safe in Japanese hands. Reforms to all of these are under way but face the typical silo mentality of a huge, powerful bureaucracy like Japan's.

Some have argued for the establishment of a joint command centre with US forces, but this is unlikely to happen in the near future, if at all: at their summit in Washington DC, on 10 April 2024, President Joe Biden and Prime Minister Kishida announced plans to reform the command-and-control structure used by US forces in Japan and to explore how to improve coordination with the JSDF, but not joint command.[27] It is too politically sensitive. Japanese and US forces already share bases and so are used to sharing information and coordinating operations, albeit not in wartime. The JMSDF is very accustomed to operating jointly with other navies, whether in exercises or in anti-piracy operations, and considers that it already operates in accordance with NATO procedures. That is less true of the other services.

Perhaps the biggest unanswered question is whether Japan can build a domestic defence industry that can develop and maintain domestic technologies, and can create a strong enough supply chain for ammunition and materials. While this will be assisted by the 2024 reforms to defence-export guidelines, it also depends on breaking down barriers between civil and military research inside universities and other institutions; this may be aided by the planned establishment of a new government research facility to be modelled on America's Defense Advanced Research Projects Agency, the famous DARPA.

It is a lot to do, in a short time, amid regional tensions and a scarcity of labour in Japan because of its ageing and shrinking population. Yet in terms of a contribution to deterrence, what matters is not whether all this can be achieved at once but rather the very clear direction of travel: Japan has declared that it intends to turn itself into a military power to be reckoned with; that it is adjusting the deployment of its forces and communications infrastructure so as to extend their reach closer to Taiwan; that it is acquiring an immediate LACM force as well as working to develop more advanced missiles; and that it intends to take on more responsibility for defending its own territory in order not to have to rely inordinately on the Americans.

As with any big programme of public spending there are always questions of how it is to be paid for, especially as

Japan's public debt in 2024 is equivalent to more than 250% of its GDP.[28] But Japan's political stability, combined with a remarkable record of monetary stability, make it safest to assume that future governments will continue to give defence a high priority and be able to finance it.

Japan is also consistent in the fact that it is carrying out this defence transformation under the same constitutional constraints that the Americans themselves imposed on it during the post-war occupation, constraints that are unlikely to change. Nonetheless, Japan's geographical position makes it exceptionally aware of the importance of Taiwan, its nearest southwestern neighbour, and of preventing any country from controlling the sea lanes along these parts of the Western Pacific. Japan's narrative about Taiwan, its former colony and one with which it maintains far friendlier relations than it does with South Korea, is close to that of the US: it adheres to the 'One China' policy by recognising that the government in Beijing is the only legitimate ruler of China, but takes no official position on whether Taiwan forms part of that One China. Japanese politicians are, if anything, more frequent visitors to Taipei than are their US equivalents: more than 40 LDP parliamentarians attended the 2023 National Day events in Taipei, for example.

In addition, Japan is playing an important part in regional diplomacy, aimed at extending the network of alliances and partnerships in the Indo-Pacific, as well as in strengthening the regional economy of Southeast Asia through its public and private investments. In 2023 it established the Official Security Assistance scheme, a new aid programme to support Southeast Asian countries' military and coastguard capabilities, and signed Reciprocal Access Agreements with both Australia and the UK to allow each other's armed forces to visit and train together more easily.[29] And it has taken a prime position in the negotiation of regional rules for trade and investment by working with Australia to revive and eventually establish the Comprehensive and Progressive Agreement for Trans-Pacific Partnership (CPTPP) for 11 Indo-Pacific countries. This group does not include the US, thanks to US domestic politics, but during 2023 it grew to 12, when the UK became the first non-Indo-Pacific country to be admitted. Partners can come from far and wide.

CHAPTER EIGHT

The Philippines, Australia and other partners

China and the United States both frequently claim that they do not want to force countries to choose sides. Nonetheless, they both frequently try at the very least to prevent countries from choosing the other side in preference to them. Neither country is particularly popular in the Indo-Pacific since both are widely perceived as being bullies. Given that it has been growing vastly in wealth and military power during the past three decades, for most countries in the Indo-Pacific, China is the neighbourhood bully whose wrath they fear while also being an unavoidable regional reality they need to come to terms with and make the best of. America, in contrast, is the distant bully on the other side of the Pacific, one that is often more resented for its neglect of the region than for throwing its weight around, though historically it has been known to do both. It is wanted in the region for its economic weight – which the toxic domestic US politics of trade have led it largely to withhold in recent years – but also as a counterbalance against Chinese domination. This is what has given America the opportunity to expand its network of allies and partners, in support of its strategy of integrated deterrence.

History had already given the US a strong starting point in the region, thanks to its series of post-war treaty-based security alliances – with Australia, Japan, New Zealand, the Philippines, South Korea and Thailand – although history and geography have left some of those alliances far stronger and more meaningful than others. Distant New Zealand, for example, no longer collaborates with the US on security under their 1951 ANZUS Treaty, but they do form part of the 'Five Eyes' intelligence-sharing network made up of Australia, Canada, New Zealand, the United Kingdom and the US.[1] Thailand has been a treaty ally of the US since 1954 and continues to receive military aid and training, but since the Vietnam War has not been a particularly close partner.[2]

Apart from Japan, the main progress the US has made in establishing a network of regional allies has come from Australia and the Philippines, with European NATO allies playing rather more distant supporting roles. A major target of diplomacy has been India, itself a would-be superpower and one that has substantial border disputes with China. Yet although America has improved its relations with India now that following withdrawal from Afghanistan it no longer also feels the need to court India's greatest foe, Pakistan, and together with Australia and Japan has successfully brought India into the Quadrilateral Security Dialogue (the Quad), there is no serious likelihood of any true military partnership. India wishes to stand on its own, joining both Chinese and US-led institutions but becoming committed to neither. At present, it is therefore of limited relevance to considerations of deterrence.

Australia and the Philippines are the countries that are most relevant to deterrence so this chapter will concentrate on them. But there is also an organisation, of which the Philippines is a member, which lies at the centre of all questions surrounding the South China Sea and hence also Taiwan, which claims 'centrality' as its objective, and yet in security matters is conspicuous by its non-centrality: the Association of Southeast Asian Nations (ASEAN). It cannot and will not be central now or any time soon. Yet looking further ahead, its ability to play a role might well grow.

The Philippines as an unsinkable logistics centre

The Philippines is, however, central geographically, in terms of its own security interests and in terms of US integrated deterrence. Here the critical question is about consistency, given the vagaries of Philippine politics. Under the presidency of Rodrigo Duterte in 2016–22 the Philippines appeared to be turning its back on the US and trying to strike bargains with China. Now, under Duterte's successor, Ferdinand R. Marcos Jr, who was elected in May 2022, the Philippines has swung strongly back towards the US. There is no way of predicting how Philippine politics and policy might swing again after President Marcos's six-year term ends in 2028.

There has, however, been a bit more consistency than presidential politics might suggest. The basic framework connecting the US and the Philippines is the Mutual Defense Treaty the two signed in 1951, five years after the Philippines gained its independence from the US following half a century of American colonial rule. The treaty requires each country to support the other if they are attacked. The US no longer has the huge military bases that it had in the Philippines during the Vietnam War and up to the early 1990s. Threats were made during the Duterte presidency that the Philippines might withdraw from a Visiting Forces Agreement the two countries still had, and even potentially from the Mutual Defense Treaty, and that joint military exercises might cease. But those threats were not carried out. And this left intact a deal that had been signed in 2014 between then-presidents Noynoy Aquino and Barack

Obama called the Enhanced Defense Cooperation Agreement (EDCA), under which the US would not maintain military bases in the Philippines but would be allowed to build facilities at Philippine military bases for both countries to use, to pre-position equipment and supplies there, and to rotate forces through those bases and facilities.

During the Duterte presidency, development of these so-called EDCA sites was largely suspended, although the Philippine armed forces improved the infrastructure at several of them during those years. Since Marcos took office in 2022, however, development at the five original sites has accelerated, with the US getting involved directly, and four more have been added.[3] Furthermore, in May 2023 the defence secretaries of the two countries signed new Bilateral Defense Guidelines to govern broader collaboration between their armed forces. Most notably, the new guidelines reaffirmed that:

> An armed attack in the Pacific, including anywhere in the South China Sea, on either of their public vessels, aircraft, or armed forces – which includes their Coast Guards – would invoke mutual defense commitments under Articles IV and V of the 1951 U.S.–Philippines Mutual Defense Treaty.[4]

This reiterated a commitment originally made in 1999 and then reaffirmed in 2019 by then-US secretary of state Michael Pompeo that the 1951 treaty did indeed cover attacks on Philippine forces in the South China Sea.[5]

This is important because close encounters are happening regularly between Chinese naval and coastguard vessels and Philippine ones in disputed areas of the South China Sea. The Philippines' effort to resolve a dispute with China over the status of islands and shoals in the Spratly Islands through the

Permanent Court of Arbitration in the Hague under the UN Convention on the Law of the Sea (UNCLOS) succeeded in court in 2016 but has been ignored by China.[6] The most recent maritime encounters have been at the Second Thomas Shoal, where the Philippines has maintained its claim to the area by keeping forces on a Philippine naval ship, the *Sierra Madre*, which it grounded on the shoal in 1999, and which it supplies by sending in other vessels that Chinese boats try to obstruct or intimidate. In December 2023, one of these encounters led to a collision between a civilian supply vessel and a Chinese coastguard ship.[7] It is possible that, thanks to those confrontations and now to America's formal commitment, an attack on a Philippine vessel by a Chinese one could become a dangerous flashpoint between US and Chinese military forces, conceivably when one side deliberately decides to test the other's resolve.

China's own actions in the South China Sea are for the time being encouraging the Philippines to draw closer to the US. What is striking is that even during the Duterte presidency, the People's Republic of China (PRC) showed little interest in seducing the Philippines to come closer to China in any serious or sustained way. Defence officials in Manila now say that it delivered on barely 5% of the investments and other goodies that were promised.[8] That may be an exaggeration reflecting President Marcos's change of tack, but even if the reality was four or five times larger it would still indicate a lack of interest, or perhaps belief, on the part of China that the Philippines would really be seducible, or worth seducing.

What the Philippines does not have, however, is a large or well-equipped military force. Between 2019 and 2023 its defence budget fluctuated between 1.4% and 1.8% of GDP, which is between US$5.3 billion and US$7.1bn in US dollar terms.[9] That is why America, under those Bilateral Defense Guidelines, is stepping up training and joint exercises, and why Japan has made the Philippines the first recipient of grants for building defence capacity under its new Official Security Assistance scheme.[10]

The main asset the Philippines is set to provide, however, is logistical support, through those nine EDCA bases. In the event of a conflict, such logistical facilities, on islands conveniently just south of Taiwan and adjacent to the South China Sea, could prove valuable, if the Philippines allows them to be used. As long as there is no future rupture between Washington DC and Manila, knowledge in China of that US logistical advantage will have some deterrent value.

Australia: far away but now committed

If you ask anyone in the French government whether the Australians should be expected to meet the test of consistency in their defence strategy, the answer may not be very polite.[11] In 2016 France signed a deal with Australia to supply it with a fleet of 12 diesel-powered submarines, under then-prime minister Malcolm Turnbull. In 2021 his successor, Scott Morrison, scrapped that deal in favour of the AUKUS 'enhanced security partnership' with the US and the UK, which will enable Australia to acquire or build a fleet of 'at least eight' nuclear-propelled submarines.[12] The following year Morrison's successor, Anthony Albanese, agreed to pay Naval Group, the French firm that had been due to supply the diesel-powered fleet, the fairly spectacular sum of €555 million (US$584m) in compensation for the scrapping of the contract.[13]

Given that the Australian government's 2020 Defence Strategic Update set its strategic objectives for defence planning as being 'to **shape** Australia's security environment; to **deter** actions against Australia's interests; and to **respond** with credible military force, when required' (bold in original text), the impression given of political indecision and disputation, and of a willingness to annoy a fellow Pacific power, France, will in the short term have undermined all three key phrases of shaping, deterring and responding.[14] But these are long-term plans and commitments, so the more important question is whether AUKUS will serve these objectives during the next several decades.

Following this chopping and changing, it must be considered unlikely that future Australian governments will want to change course again, unless some major problems arise in AUKUS and in its programme to develop and build the nuclear-propelled submarines, or unless the cost to the public purse becomes unbearable. In theory, however, the chopping and changing could come from a future US or British government, rather than an Australian one, if either were to take the view that AUKUS had become a bad deal for them. The trigger that could prompt this in America could be concern that the US fleet of attack submarines has become too small, and new production too slow, for America to afford to allocate any of those submarines for early transfer to Australia, as is potentially provided for in AUKUS.[15] As Nick Childs, IISS Senior Fellow for Naval Forces and Maritime Security, wrote in his article in the journal *Survival*, 'AUKUS has long been recognised as a high-reward, high-risk enterprise', and it is one that depends vitally on trust given that this is the first time the US has agreed to share its nuclear-propulsion technology with another ally since it did so for the UK in 1958.[16]

In practice, the three partners in AUKUS will have many opportunities to adjust and renegotiate aspects of the programme's schedule and provisions. A full break-up of AUKUS would be likely to arise only in the event of a wider schism in the overall Western alliance, one which led all parties to distrust each other sufficiently to forgo the benefits of collaboration. That is where the high risks arise from: this is a multi-decade agreement, which is naturally vulnerable to the fluctuations of domestic politics in all three countries and in international relations.

Notwithstanding those risks, from a deterrence point of view it is best to focus on what the high rewards might consist of and ask how they might serve the interests of the US-led Western alliance, which could potentially be a factor in making that alliance resilient to political fluctuations. Chapter Four touched upon these: well before Australia's new nuclear-propelled submarines come into service, the AUKUS arrangement has enabled the US to increase further its use of Australian bases.

Since the Obama administration's 'pivot to Asia' in 2014, Australia has hosted up to 2,500 US troops and some military aircraft at Darwin.[17] The distance between Darwin and Taiwan (4,160 kilometres) limits the value of those forces in deterring an invasion or blockade of Taiwan. However, the creation under the AUKUS umbrella of Submarine Rotational Force–West, expected to be constituted from 2027 by 'up to four' US nuclear-powered submarines and one from the Royal Navy, and based at HMAS Stirling in Perth, can make a serious contribution in supporting the ability to respond at speed and scale to an attempted invasion of Taiwan.[18]

Along with Taiwan's own new diesel-powered submarines and with other US submarines sailing from Guam, this force will raise important questions in the minds of Chinese military planners about undersea attacks on any invasion force – at least until or unless undersea-surveillance technologies advance so rapidly in the People's Liberation Army (PLA) Navy as to outpace the evasion capabilities of US submarines. That worry about future technological obsolescence may be greater for Australia's new submarines, due as they are to be developed and built for entry into service in both the British and Australian navies in the late 2030s and early 2040s.

Questions about how well Australia's narratives on China, Taiwan and the status quo align with those of its allies are harder to pin down, for they are also subject to political fluctuations and debate. For decades, it sought a close relationship with China, the main market for its iron ore and other commodities.[19] Australia has become strongly aligned with the American view on China's general threat only since 2020, when calls for an inquiry into the origins of COVID-19 by then-prime minister Morrison and then his public criticisms of the National Security Law in Hong Kong led to China publishing '14 grievances' against Australia and then imposing tariffs and boycotts on some major Australian exports to China. Despite China being Australia's biggest trading partner, Australia weathered three years of such economic coercion well.[20] The country has also been at the forefront of countering what it sees as Chinese influence operations in its domestic politics and academia. For the time being, this has aligned Australia's narrative on deterrence and regional security closely with that of the US, which helped make the AUKUS decision politically viable. Prime Minister Albanese's keynote address to the IISS Shangri-La Dialogue in June 2023 contained this particularly resonant passage:

> In boosting our nation's defence capability, Australia's goal is not to prepare for war, but to prevent it through deterrence and reassurance and building resilience in the region, doing our part to fulfil the shared responsibility all of us have to preserve peace and security. And making it crystal clear that when it comes to any unilateral attempt to change the status quo by force, be it in Taiwan, the South China Sea, the East China Sea or elsewhere, the risk of conflict will always far outweigh any potential reward.[21]

Other allies and bystanders, near and far

In the American catalogue of allies and partners in the Indo-Pacific there is a long list of other countries beyond those already surveyed: South Korea, the United States' other close security-treaty ally; Vietnam, with which it established a Comprehensive Strategic Partnership in September 2023; Indonesia, with which it holds the annual *Garuda Shield* military exercises together with Japan, Australia and other allies; and last but not least Singapore, where since a 1990 memorandum of understanding the US military has been able to use the country's air and naval bases on a non-exclusive basis, and which has been a major customer for F-16 and now F-35 fighter jets, the training of pilots for which takes place at US bases in Arizona and soon in Arkansas.[22] To those can be added European NATO member countries, principally France, Germany, the Netherlands and the UK, which have been sending naval vessels alone or as collaborators in carrier strike groups to the Indo-Pacific for joint exercises and for freedom-of-navigation operations.

The length of this list, and the fact that the number of countries seeking friendly if loose relations with the US is growing rather than shrinking, has some deterrent value: the message it sends is that any idea of Chinese maritime hegemony over the South China and East China seas remains contested. In terms of regional diplomacy and, especially, of collaborative efforts to set rules governing the free flow of trade and investment, Japan plays a much bigger role than does the US. Due to the hostility to free-trade deals that has taken hold in the US Congress, the US has been unable to offer much to the region since 2017, when president Donald Trump withdrew the US from the Trans-Pacific Partnership (TPP) trade agreement that his predecessor, Obama, had initiated and negotiated with 11 other countries. Yet having Japan take the lead, as it did along with Australia in reviving and reconstituting the TPP as the Comprehensive and

Progressive Agreement for Trans-Pacific Partnership (CPTPP) in 2018, now being joined by the UK, makes a lot of sense. Japan knows the region far better than does the US, and through the CPTPP and other forums can be in much closer and more regular contact with Southeast Asian governments than the US can.

In terms of the direct deterrence of a conflict over Taiwan, and of the cataclysmic broader war that such a conflict could readily lead to, these relationships cannot play a big role. The European NATO countries are too far away to be able to offer the threat of a speedy response, even if they could well play an important part in a protracted conflict.[23] This applies even to France, which although it can and does claim to be a Pacific power currently has its Pacific possessions and military assets too far away to make a rapid difference. South Korea knows it is in the American camp in order to deter and potentially fight North Korea and is becoming an increasingly important arms supplier both within the region and outside it, but even current right-wing President Yoon Suk-yeol prefers to avoid confronting China directly and has stayed deafeningly silent about Taiwan. The defeat President Yoon's party suffered in legislative elections in April 2024 will further discourage him from being too active.[24] Indonesia, Singapore, Thailand and Vietnam are all members of the Southeast Asian camp that is vocal about not wanting to be in anyone's camp: all are keen on persuading and enabling America to maintain its presence in the region as a counterbalance to China, but none wants to be seen as an American ally.

For the purposes of affecting the psychology of Chinese military planners or political leaders, the only countries that can in advance be considered 'probables' as participants in an intervention to defend Taiwan alongside the US are Japan and Australia, with the Philippines and its logistics facilities next as a 'possible', subject to domestic politics at the time. South Korea might feel forced to end its studied neutrality over

Taiwan out of fear that Taiwan's fall could threaten its own security, but this cannot be relied upon. European NATO allies can be seen as 'probable moral supporters' that would be too far away to make a difference in the short term but would be assumed by Chinese planners to be likely to fight alongside the US if a full-scale war were to ensue. India and the other Southeast Asian countries should be considered 'unlikelies'. That is not surprising in India's case, for however much richer and more powerful that country may become by the middle of this century, its geography will always make it somewhat politically separated from events in the South China Sea.

ASEAN non-centrality

The anomalous countries, however, are the other Southeast Asian states, for geography gives them a deep and permanent interest in peace and security in their region. That is a good reason not to want to choose sides between China and the US. Whether it can remain a good reason not to play a bigger role themselves in shaping their own security environment is now under question, however. In the past, they have generally felt too weak and poor to be able to stand up for themselves on security, with a large and until recently widening imbalance of economic and military power between them and China. But this could change over the next few decades, and to some degree is already beginning to do so.

Indonesia, the largest Southeast Asian country in terms of population, currently ranks number 16 in the world in terms of GDP at market exchange rates, far behind China, which ranks second to the US. As befits its 2024 population of 279.8m,[25] Indonesia's armed forces are the second largest in numerical terms in Southeast Asia with 404,500 personnel in active service.[26] But its defence budget in 2023 was US$8.7bn, just 0.63% of GDP. Spending money on defence has not been a priority. That may in part reflect Indonesia's own history and the role played by its military forces before 1998 when Suharto, the long-time dictator, was overthrown and democracy was re-established. But it also reflects a decision to focus on domestic affairs, to keep its head down and to channel much of its foreign-policy energy through ASEAN.

The other nine members of ASEAN – Brunei, Cambodia, Laos, Malaysia, Myanmar, the Philippines, Singapore, Thailand and Vietnam – are less parsimonious on defence, but most (with the notable exception of Singapore) focus chiefly on internal security. Only Brunei, Cambodia, Myanmar and Singapore spend more than 2% of their annual GDP on defence, and only Singapore has managed to join the ranks of the world's wealthiest countries.[27] That wealth allowed Singapore's annual defence budget to be US$13.4bn in 2023, or 2.7% of GDP, which is by far the largest in ASEAN and is more than 50% larger than that of Indonesia, a country with 50 times its population (see Figure 5).[28]

This economic and political reality, when placed amid the contested geography of the South China Sea and the great-power

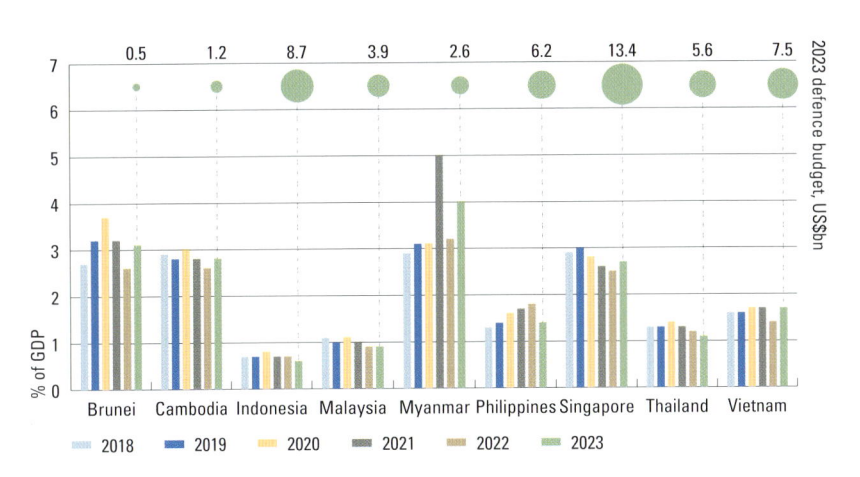

Figure 5: **Defence spending of ASEAN member countries, 2018–23**

Note: No data available for Laos.
Source: IISS Military Balance+

©IISS

competition that surrounds it, helps to explain three important things. The first is a notorious remark made at the 2010 ASEAN Regional Forum meeting in Vietnam by China's then-foreign minister Yang Jiechi: 'China is a big country and other countries are small countries and that is just a fact.'[29] This is indeed a fact and in terms of maritime forces has become even more true a decade and a half later. It was not very diplomatic of Yang to say this, but that disproportion perfectly explains the PRC's conduct at that time in the South China Sea, where it was beginning to reclaim land to build military facilities, was ignoring ASEAN countries' exclusive economic zones when it suited, and was pressing its claim to the whole South China Sea inside the 'nine-dash line' first promulgated by Chiang Kai-shek with 11 'dashes' in 1948.[30] That claim, it was stated in the 2016 decision by the Permanent Court of Arbitration in The Hague in the case brought by the Philippines over the Scarborough Shoal, has no legal basis under UNCLOS. China has signed and ratified UNCLOS but has nevertheless ignored the 2016 ruling. The US signed UNCLOS but has never ratified it.[31]

The second thing it explains is the fact that this conduct has continued ever since, with increased clashes as the PLA Navy and coastguard fleet have grown, and yet no progress at all has been achieved on a project ASEAN has been discussing with China ever since 1996: the drawing up of a 'Code of Conduct' for maritime operations in the South China Sea. Having in 2002 agreed with China a non-binding but bland 'Declaration on the Conduct of Parties in the South China Sea', it was only 21 years later in July 2023 that ASEAN finally managed to strike an agreement with the PRC not on the Code of Conduct itself but on 'guidelines' for how talks on that Code are to be managed.[32]

This slow progress can be attributed in part to the fact that only four of the ten ASEAN member states hold official claims to the waters and features in the South China Sea that is disputed with China – Malaysia, Vietnam, the Philippines and Brunei. Indonesia and Singapore are not claimants but have expressed concerns. But the slow progress also must be attributed to the disparities in power that Yang pointed out, and the fact that there has been no progress on claims clarifications and negotiations under UNCLOS among the different Southeast Asian claimants themselves, let alone with the PRC.

As a result, the third important thing that this economic and political reality explains is why the term 'ASEAN centrality', which is rooted in the organisation's charter from 2007, has become meaningless when it is applied to security issues in the South China Sea or in the wider Indo-Pacific.[33] Centrality is supposed to mean that this organisation expects to be at the heart of the discussion of any regional issue. ASEAN's recent 'Outlook on the Indo-Pacific' says that it 'envisages ASEAN Centrality as the underlying principle for promoting cooperation in the Indo-Pacific region', and that it will 'undertake cooperation in a broad range of areas, including … unresolved maritime disputes that have the potential for open conflict'.[34]

The trouble is that no one else, most notably China, believes this to be either true or realistic, however often diplomats invoke ASEAN centrality in their speeches.[35] Or, to put it another way, China's actions in dividing ASEAN when it wishes to and in ignoring it when it sees fit, suggest that it simply accords ASEAN a central role in being bulldozed aside. It is a big country, and they are smaller ones, and that is a fact, even when they are grouped in an association.

Limits to the ASEAN way

That association has been remarkably successful at achieving the fundamental and original goal for which it was created in 1967: resolving or avoiding disputes between its members. The forum it provides has established the habit and obligation of mutual consultation and communication, but without countenancing direct intervention in the internal affairs of any member state and without setting up a central body with the power or means to enforce rulings or make interventions. This occasionally produces bouts of frustration and soul-searching, especially of late over the 2021 military coup and subsequent civil war in Myanmar. Internal critics, such as Malaysia ahead of the annual ASEAN summit in September 2023, call for tougher action over Myanmar but then fail to get it.[36]

More objectively, what that failure is proof of is not relevance or otherwise but the priority ASEAN and its member governments have given to the forum's own survival rather than to any goals of operational effectiveness. Nor, especially once the initial five-country ASEAN was enlarged to include first Brunei, then Vietnam, and finally the very different and weaker states of Laos, Myanmar and Cambodia, has there been any sustained effort to agree upon a meaningful, shared set of principles or values beyond what the former Singaporean diplomat Kishore Mahbubani rightly calls 'a culture of pragmatism and accommodation'.[37]

That culture has accompanied healthy economic growth for most – though not all –ASEAN members and booming trade with China. This trading boom is just as it should be given that China and Southeast Asia are neighbours and that so long as barriers between them are lowered, as they have been through successive trade deals – most recently the Regional Comprehensive Economic Partnership – neighbours are always natural trading partners.[38] But regarding the South China Sea through which that goods trade flows, their economic and political weakness has meant that 'accommodation' has simply meant having to stand by while China does what it pleases. As with other large associations of nations – the 27-member European Union is a prime example – it is extremely hard for

ASEAN to make collective decisions about controversial issues, a category in which dealing with China is always going to fit.

None of this is likely to change in the short or medium term. Whatever one thinks about the institutions or governments involved, the fundamental reality is of a huge imbalance in political and military power between China and its ASEAN neighbours. That imbalance explains why many Southeast Asian countries remain eager to ensure that America retains its military presence in the region, while seeking to avoid being seen as members of one camp or another.

Another emerging solution is to increase the use of 'minilaterals' (i.e., collaborations between smaller groups of member countries) to try to make progress on security issues. In early 2024 Indonesia, the Philippines and Vietnam held a series of high-level bilateral summits to discuss security cooperation.[39] If continued and turned into practical arrangements, this cooperation would strengthen the ability of those big littoral nations to resist Chinese bullying outside the ASEAN framework. Nonetheless, until all three countries feel able and willing to spend more on defence, the basic imbalance between their power and that of China will remain.

Dreaming of a more balanced region

One change that has occurred in recent years is that the pace of economic growth in China has slowed while the pace of growth in many of the countries around its borders has accelerated. Whereas for the past two decades or more China has played both a central and a leading role in generating economic growth in Asia, now much of Southeast and South Asia is matching or even outpacing it. The leader in this is India, but also closer to home annual growth rates of 5–8% have begun to be recorded in Indonesia, Malaysia, the Philippines and Vietnam.

To expect all those four countries to achieve and sustain annual average growth rates over the next two decades at the level China did since 2000 looks courageous, to say the least. Nonetheless, it is worth recalling how much progress China made in those two decades, during which it achieved annual average economic-growth rates at or close to 8%: at the start of the new millennium, China's defence budget was ranked fourth in the world, behind Japan's, and its economy was merely the world's sixth largest.[40] Now, China is the world's second-largest economy and accordingly can afford a vastly bigger defence budget, which now ranks second in the world.

What if some of the populous Southeast Asian nations were to do the same during the next quarter-century? A simple calculation can illustrate what could happen if such Chinese-style growth rates could be replicated.

Indonesia's GDP in 2023 was US$1.5 trillion, while those of Malaysia, the Philippines and Vietnam were all around US$400–450bn.[41] If we combine those to form one economy with a GDP of US$2.7trn and apply a compounded annual growth rate of 7% between now and 2050, the outcome would be a combined GDP of approximately US$18trn in that year. Indonesia's GDP alone would reach nearly US$8trn if it were to achieve 7% annual average growth over that quarter-century.

China's GDP in 2022 totalled US$17.5trn. Let us assume that it will continue to grow, but that the burdens of demography, maturity and rigidity reduce the pace of that growth to something closer to European or American levels. If we apply a compounded annual growth rate of 3% a year over that period to that starting number, China's GDP would reach approximately US$40trn in 2050.

These calculations show that if our combined Indonesia–Malaysia–Philippines–Vietnam economy were to achieve a China-like annual average growth rate of 7% while China's slowed to 3%, then the GDP of the combined four would by 2050 have risen to 45% of that of China from about 15% now. This is just pure arithmetic, which takes no account of inflation or of exchange-rate movements. The idea that all four countries, with their different political dynamics, could sustain such rapid growth throughout such a long period without bumps and crises is far-fetched. But some of them could likely get close, while China's growth too could be bumpier than in the past.

The fundamental point is that the current huge imbalance between China's economic and political power and that of its neighbours around the South China Sea is neither immutable nor permanent. ASEAN's big nations have the potential to become a lot more powerful, to be able to afford bigger and more effective defence budgets, and then to be able to exercise more individual and collective influence over regional security. If that happens, then partnerships and alliances between and with those countries will also become vitally important, especially for Japan if it really wants to deter China and to protect its own security.

That, however, is a dream for the decades to come. The principal concerns about deterrence need addressing much more urgently than that.

CONCLUSION

Nostalgic for Cold War realism

The clue to the most important fact about the Cold War is contained in its name: there was no 'hot' conflict between the superpowers during that long confrontation from about 1947 to 1991. Their ideological differences were fundamental and their suspicions of each other were powerful, and there were proxy wars aplenty. Nuclear weapons would have meant that had a war between the West and the USSR taken place, the result could have been the destruction of much of the planet. Once this was understood, two big things happened. Firstly, both sides built up their military forces and tried to get ahead of the other in terms of military technology and to seek advantage in all sorts of ways; and secondly, after an initial decade and a half of unbridled competition, the two sides negotiated a series of agreements and treaties designed to make this competition more transparent, more constrained and, above all, better understood by both sides. The clearest feature of all during the Cold War was the realisation that the gravest danger lay in a misunderstanding by one side of the actions, motivations or likely responses of the other. Hence the mutual recognition of the need for clarity, even while both sides were engaged in all sorts of lower-level subterfuge, secrecy and skulduggery.[1]

That danger remains valid today, even in a world that is more complicated and in which, thanks to satellite and other digital technology, the United States and China know a lot more about each other than did America and the Soviet Union in the early years of the nuclear age. What they do not understand well is each other's motivations, ambitions or likely responses. Part of the reason is that motivations, ambitions and responses are matters of psychology, not of statistics or pure military strengths, and so are far harder to detect, let alone interpret. The other part is that psychology is changeable, especially when political leaderships change. Without consistency and clarity there cannot be stability, for all sides have an incentive to look for opportunities to gain an advantage each time the other side's attitudes seem cast into doubt.

As a result, the dangers of a catastrophic war breaking out – a war in which nuclear weapons would be likelier to play a part than not – are higher than at any time since at least the Cuban Missile Crisis of 1962, but probably since the end of the Korean War in 1953. The stakes are high: along with symbolically declaring a belated victory in its twentieth-century wars by absorbing Taiwan, China would clearly like to gain maritime control over the Western Pacific, and its route to doing so would be to capture Taiwan and thereby to drive US forces out of the region. The US would very much like to prevent this, because it would likely destroy all its security alliances in the region, would push it back to Guam, Hawaii and even to its mainland, and would put in danger the free and safe movement of ships, aircraft and people. It would also place a successful democracy, which the US has been supporting for three-quarters of a century, into the hands of a dictatorship, and would place America's long-time allies – notably Japan, the Philippines and South Korea – in a strategically parlous position. This would mark the end of the US as a global power.

This *Adelphi* book has attempted to map the way in which many countries in and outside the Indo-Pacific region are working hard to try to reduce the risks of that catastrophic war happening, and to evaluate their efforts. What is being constructed amounts to a matrix of deterrence strategies: above all the rival efforts by China, the US and Taiwan; but also the active and important involvement of Australia, Japan, the Philippines and a host of supporting actors in America's strategy. Much of these attempts at deterrence are by physical means, an arms race if you will, with defence spending having risen rapidly in China, Japan and Taiwan; with American, Australian and Japanese force postures becoming more forward-leaning and deterrent in intent; with logistical networks being reinforced and extended by Japan, the Philippines and the US; and with military exercises and air and sea incursions being used in demonstrative ways by both China and the US.

A significant part of those competitive efforts at deterrence is also taking place in the form of rival narratives: between a 'free and open Indo-Pacific' and the opposing idea of Asian security being just a matter for Asians; between Taiwan as an 'internal matter' for the Chinese people to resolve and the notion of Taiwan as both a regional and global concern over stability, human rights and maritime control; between rival interpretations of history and of the weight it carries in international law; and between differing conceptions of which powers are disruptors and which are stabilisers.

That contest of narratives is interesting and inevitable, but also exposes the acute danger of a misunderstanding about the most fundamental and obvious issue of all: that of whether a conflict over Taiwan can be defined and constrained as a local and conventional affair, or whether it needs to be thought of as unavoidably global in its implications and potentially nuclear. The costs and risks of a local, conventional war might seem acceptable; the costs and risks of a global, even nuclear one should not be acceptable to anyone, even to a side that thinks it could come out the winner.

Needed: the good aspect of Cold War diplomacy

The simplest truth about deterrence is that whether you define it as being by 'denial' or by 'punishment', or whether you elevate it to the mutually assured destruction threats of the Cold War, in the end it is founded on psychology. To cite Lawrence Freedman again, 'it is about setting boundaries for actions', but to set those boundaries requires the adversary's psychology to be susceptible to your threats and requires the adversary to believe that you really intend, and really will be able, to carry out those threats.[2]

The inescapable conclusion from this author's research into the deterrence strategies of all the parties in the Indo-Pacific whose interests encircle Taiwan and the China seas is that, impressive as many of them are, they cannot be fully convincing. We can never be sure of what effect they will have on the calculations of an adversary whose motivations and perceptions of their own interest must ultimately remain uncertain. This applies most clearly to the calculations of China and to the thinking of a long-serving dictatorial leader such as Xi Jinping, who like Vladimir Putin brooks no dissent and is likely to receive an increasingly narrow input of information. But it also applies to Chinese calculations about America: efforts to gauge the priority really ascribed to defending Taiwan and to assess the political will really held by whoever is in the White House at a moment of crisis, can only ever be educated guesswork. Moreover, this is not a danger belonging to a particular moment in time: as far as we can tell, it is a perpetual one.

In that sense, but only that sense, we are back in the conditions of the first decades of the Cold War. To describe today's world as being in a broad sense in 'a new Cold War' is wrong, or at least highly misleading: whatever measures both sides have taken to reduce economic and technological dependencies on the other, whether through 'decoupling' or 'de-risking' of supply chains and financial connections, what is notable is that the interconnections between these two huge economies have so far remained strong and extensive, and that both have their own interconnections with most other economies. The world has not become divided into two clear blocs, as it was during the real Cold War. It remains highly connected, and the connections are intricate. Only a hot war would truly drive us apart – and the lack of understanding of each other and of each other's motivations is both the biggest risk that this could happen and the one true parallel with the original Cold War.

This lack of mutual understanding, or at least of the clear communication that facilitates such understanding, gains particular importance if we start to think about the role of nuclear weapons in a potential US–China conflict. As during the Cold War, it is possible to conceive of such a conflict remaining one that purely uses conventional weapons, and it can even be argued that the mutual possession of nuclear arsenals might lead both sides to seek to keep any conflict limited, even in the case of quite a protracted war.[3] But should these possibilities be relied upon, given the consequences if the conflict were to turn nuclear?

There are plenty of technical reasons for not relying on this notion: being sure that one's conflict with another nuclear power will remain a so-called limited war raises all sorts of military difficulties. The far bigger reason, however, is political. Whichever way you look at it, the politics of deciding to fight a limited war against a fellow nuclear power look perilous. Who wants to be the political leader who chooses to fight a conventional war that then turns nuclear, destroying much of his or her own country? Who wants to be the political leader who loses a conventional war because of an unwillingness to use nuclear weapons? That leader might certainly think afterwards that it would have been better to have made a clear nuclear threat in advance to stop the war from starting in the first place. It may be conceivable that a future US–China war could remain limited and conventional, but is it likely? And what if that conception proves wrong?

Writing with the hindsight of 2005 but naturally not the foresight of the 2020s, the doyen of Cold War historians, John Lewis Gaddis, averred that:

> J. Robert Oppenheimer ... predicted in 1946 that 'if there is another major war, atomic weapons will be used'. The man who ran the program that built the bomb had the logic right, but the Cold War inverted it: what happened instead was that because nuclear weapons *could* be used in any new great power war, no such war took place.[4]

The critical deterrence question about a US–China war is that, to paraphrase Gaddis, since nuclear weapons *could* be used, can the terrible prospect for all sides of that use be turned into a monumental obstacle to any such war ever taking place, as it was (with hindsight) during the Cold War?

A sea change in the level of diplomatic and thus political clarity would be required to get to that point. As things stand, there is no such clarity about whether whoever the leaders of China and the US are at the time would be willing to use nuclear weapons in a war that begins over Taiwan, nor over the disposition and nature of China's nuclear forces.

During the Cold War, the achievement of that clarity was begun, essentially, by the Cuban Missile Crisis of 1962, in which an episode rife with misunderstandings about each side's intentions towards an island close to one of them gave rise to a process of diplomacy and negotiation. That process, which began with the Limited Test Ban Treaty of 1963 and passed through the Nuclear Non-Proliferation Treaty (1968), the Strategic Arms Limitation Treaty I (Interim Agreement – 1972) and onward into further arms-control agreements, combined hard engagement on the most critical issue between the two superpowers – nuclear weapons, in all their aspects – with a consistent political focus on the behaviour and apparent intentions of counterpart leaders. The consistency and evident existential importance of this engagement also contributed to the generally bipartisan and quite consistent approach to it across changing US administrations. Nonetheless, we should recall that even after the 1962 Cuba crisis had yielded a process for managing the competition, there were plenty of episodes of instability and potentially fatal misunderstandings: no process is likely to be a perfect guarantee.

There were countless bad aspects of Cold War diplomacy, but in hindsight that was the good aspect. Alongside the conventional deterrence strategies, and some of the strengthening and clarifying of nuclear deterrence through modernisation, nuclear-sharing and restated doctrines that is already under discussion, what is needed is the modern diplomatic and political equivalent of that good aspect.[5] There need not be a new Cold War, but we must learn from the old Cold War about the value of such a diplomatic framework. Currently, no such framework exists.

American and Chinese officials and even presidents do meet from time to time, of course. They discuss lots of other matters, such as climate change, trade and economics, and occasionally their military leaders meet, including annually at the IISS Shangri-La Dialogue in Singapore. But there are two gigantic holes in the current diplomacy:

- There are no arms-control agreements between China and the US (or anyone else), covering either nuclear weapons or any form of missiles, nor currently any sign from China that it is willing to countenance a substantive form of arms control.
- There has been no formal agreement between China and the US about Taiwan since the US–China Joint Communiqué of 17 August 1982. The world has changed hugely in the four decades since then, including notably in the sense that Taiwan has become a democracy but also that China has transformed itself from a military and economic weakling into a giant on both counts. The need for the US to repeat and underline the fact that it opposes a Taiwanese declaration of independence is a constant, but such reaffirmation would be made more convincing by placing it into a more modern framework than that of 1982.

In November 2023, the two sides held their first talks about arms control since the time of the Obama administration, but little of substance emerged.[6] This is likely to remain the case unless and until the top leaders (i.e., the US and Chinese presidents) succeed in convincing each other that there is something to be gained by putting lower-level officials to work at exchanging information about weapons, missiles and the rest, and exploring the scope for agreements, thus setting in train the sort of process that was such a helpful feature of Cold War diplomacy.

While China has long insisted on separating discussion of what it calls its 'core interests', in which category Taiwan certainly falls, from discussion of all other matters, including strategic stability, the hope must be that eventually this may change if successive US presidents convey convincing messages that what President Joe Biden said in 2021 and 2022 is now a firm and consistent US policy: that the US would intervene militarily in an attempted invasion or blockade of Taiwan, with the implication that in the ensuing conflict, the use of nuclear weapons cannot be ruled out. Most likely, China will never accept publicly that Taiwan is anything other than an 'internal matter' and will seek to preserve the hope that reunification could either be peaceful or achieved by conventional means, but pure self-interest will start to dictate at least a private or implied realism about the need for dialogue with the US the more it becomes clear that a Taiwan conflict holds an unavoidable risk of turning nuclear.

This realism could in fact be further assisted by China's own nuclear expansion, which currently must be counted as being only in its early stages. As American and other officials have frequently said, this expansion raises questions about nuclear doctrines, about missile-launch protocols and a host of other issues.[7] Moreover, there is plenty that needs to be talked about in other domains, notably space. As China's nuclear expansion proceeds, so it may come to believe – or be able to be convinced by other countries to believe – that the best way to deal with neighbouring countries' concerns about that expansion will be to place it in an arms-control framework, one that would have to include but need not be limited to the US. This undoubtedly will not happen tomorrow, but it can be a goal for the day after tomorrow. Such an arms-control framework need not necessarily constrain China's nuclear expansion but rather would be a process that would demand and involve greater transparency about its many aspects.

We are all deterrers now, as this *Adelphi* has sought to show, and we certainly need to be. But only once it has become clear, consistently so, that the most important level of deterrence, namely the nuclear sort, has taken its rightfully primary position in strategic thinking and in diplomatic dialogue in the Indo-Pacific, will we be able to feel reassured. Currently, war over Taiwan and hence between China and the US can be described as 'possible, avoidable, but potentially catastrophic'. This author will sleep more easily once it becomes describable by all sides as 'inevitably catastrophic and therefore inconceivable'.

NOTES

Introduction

1. Lawrence Freedman's book *Deterrence* (Cambridge: Polity Press, 2004) is the best guide this author has found to the rise and fall of this concept.
2. Charles Krauthammer, 'The Unipolar Moment', *Foreign Affairs*, 1 January 1990, https://www.foreignaffairs.com/articles/1990-01-01/unipolar-moment.
3. President of Russia, 'Joint Statement of the Russian Federation and the People's Republic of China on the International Relations Entering a New Era and the Global Sustainable Development', 4 February 2022, http://en.kremlin.ru/supplement/5770.
4. *Ibid*.
5. C. Todd Lopez, US Department of Defense, 'Defense Secretary Says "Integrated Deterrence" Is Cornerstone of US Defense', DOD News, 30 April 2021, https://www.defense.gov/News/News-Stories/Article/Article/2592149/defense-secretary-says-integrated-deterrence-is-cornerstone-of-us-defense.
6. Prime Minister's Office of Japan, 'Keynote Address by Prime Minister Kishida Fumio at the IISS Shangri-La Dialogue', 10 June 2022, https://japan.kantei.go.jp/101_kishida/statement/202206/_00002.html#:~:text=I%20will%20lay%20out%20a,cyber%20security%2C%20digital%20and%20green.
7. Brendan Taylor, *Dangerous Decade: Taiwan's Security and Crisis Management*, Adelphi 470 (Abingdon: Routledge for the IISS, 2019), p. 13.
8. *Ibid*.
9. See Henry Boyd, Franz-Stefan Gady and Meia Nouwens, 'Deterrence Failure in a Cross-strait Conflict: The Role of Alliances, Military Balance and Emerging Technology', IISS Scenario Workshop Report, February 2023, https://www.iiss.org/globalassets/pages---content--migration/blogs/research-paper/deterrence-failure-in-a-crossstrait-conflict-report.pdf; and Mark F. Cancian, Matthew Cancian and Eric Heginbotham, 'The First Battle of the Next War: Wargaming a Chinese Invasion of Taiwan', Centre for

Strategic and International Studies, 9 January 2023, https://www.csis.org/analysis/first-battle-next-war-wargaming-chinese-invasion-taiwan. Of course, there are also a number of reports or studies that do consider nuclear use (sometimes even advocating nuclear first use). See, for example, Matthew Kroenig, 'Deliberate Nuclear Use in a War Over Taiwan: Scenarios and Considerations for the United States', Scowcroft Center for Strategy and Security, Atlantic Council, September 2023, https://www.atlanticcouncil.org/wp-content/uploads/2023/10/Kroenig-Deliberate-Nuclear-Use-in-a-War-over-Taiwan.pdf.

[10] Bill Emmott, *Rivals: How the Power Struggle between China, India and Japan Will Shape Our Next Decade* (London: Allen Lane, 2008).

Chapter One

[1] 'Closer than Ever: It Is 100 Seconds to Midnight', *Bulletin of the Atomic Scientists*, January 2020, https://thebulletin.org/doomsday-clock/2020-doomsday-clock-statement/.

[2] 'A Moment of Historic Danger: It Is Still 90 Seconds to Midnight', *Bulletin of the Atomic Scientists*, January 2024, https://thebulletin.org/doomsday-clock/current-time/.

[3] Aaron Blake, 'Why Biden and the White House Keep Talking about World War III', *Washington Post*, 17 March 2022, https://www.washingtonpost.com/politics/2022/03/17/why-biden-white-house-keep-talking-about-world-war-iii/.

[4] President Joe Biden, 'Comments to the House Democratic Caucus Issues Conference', Philadelphia, 13 March 2022, https://www.bloomberg.com/news/videos/2022-03-13/world-war-iii-won-t-be-fought-in-ukraine-biden-says-video?sref=A6h4yyDS.

[5] For the texts of the US–China Joint Communiqués of 1972, 1979 and 1982, as well as the 1979 Taiwan Relations Act and the 1982 'Six Assurances' to Taiwan, see 'Taiwan: Texts of the Taiwan Relations Act, the U.S.–China Communiques, and the "Six Assurances"', Congressional Research Service Report for Congress, 21 May 1998, https://www.everycrsreport.com/files/19980521_96-246F_a5b0e9334d4b4028eeb7dcb41626bddef3dc2c9a.pdf.

[6] The convention of 'strategic ambiguity' has not been strictly adhered to by all presidents: in 2001, George W. Bush also pledged to do 'whatever it takes' to help Taiwan defend itself. See Kelly Wallace, 'Bush Pledges Whatever It Takes to Defend Taiwan', CNN, 25 April 2001, https://edition.cnn.com/2001/ALLPOLITICS/04/24/bush.taiwan.abc/. But President Biden's four statements have been the clearest and most sustained breach of that convention to date.

[7] President of Russia, 'Joint Statement of the Russian Federation and the People's Republic of China on the International Relations Entering a New Era and the Global Sustainable Development', 4 February 2022, http://en.kremlin.ru/supplement/5770.

[8] Cited in Alan D. Romberg, 'Rein In at the Brink of the Precipice: American

Policy toward Taiwan and US–PRC Relations', Henry L. Stimson Center, 2003, https://www.stimson.org/2001/rein-brink-precipice-american-policy-toward-taiwan-and-us-prc-relations/.

9   Yimou Lee, Sarah Wu and Greg Torode, 'China's Freeze on Taiwan Contact Fuels Worry as Tensions Build', Reuters, 17 November 2022, https://www.reuters.com/world/china/chinas-freeze-taiwan-contact-fuels-worry-tensions-build-2022-11-17/.

10 Russell Hsiao, 'Taiwanese Perceptions of Cross-strait Relations after the 20th CCP Congress', *Global Taiwan Brief*, vol. 7, no. 22, 16 November 2022, https://globaltaiwan.org/2022/11/taiwanese-perceptions-of-cross-strait-relations-after-the-20th-ccp-congress/.

11 Joel Guinto, 'How China Is Fighting in the Grey Zone against Taiwan', BBC News, 4 October 2023, https://www.bbc.com/news/world-asia-66851118.

12 David Sacks and Ivan Kanapathy, 'What It Will Take to Deter China in the Taiwan Strait', *Foreign Affairs*, 15 June 2023, https://www.foreignaffairs.com/china/what-it-will-take-deter-china-taiwan-strait.

13 Mallory Shelbourne, 'Davidson: China Could Try to Take Control of Taiwan in "Next Six Years"', US Naval Institute, 9 March 2021, https://news.usni.org/2021/03/09/davidson-china-could-try-to-take-control-of-taiwan-in-next-six-years.

14 Romberg, 'Rein In at the Brink of the Precipice'.

15 This old phrase predates President Xi Jinping, having first been used by president Jiang Zemin in 2001, but Xi has given it new emphasis and force.

16 For a crisp summary of the history of Chinese rule, see Rana Mitter, *Modern China: A Very Short Introduction* (Oxford: Oxford University Press, 2008), pp. 90–3. For 'inalienable part of China', see 'Explainer: Why Taiwan Is an Inalienable Part of China', CGTN, 5 August 2022, https://news.cgtn.com/news/2022-08-05/Explainer-Why-Taiwan-is-an-inalienable-part-of-China-1cfD2fT39e0/index.html.

17 Kathryn Hille, 'Becoming Taiwan: In China's Shadow, an Island Asserts Its Identity', *Financial Times*, 6 January 2023, https://www.ft.com/content/6e9a0243-87f2-445e-b563-e8f67082b3da.

18 See Mitter, *Modern China*. The Qing Dynasty lasted from 1644 to 1912.

19 Toshi Yoshihara and James R. Holmes, *Red Star Over the Pacific: China's Rise and the Challenge to US Maritime Strategy* (Annapolis, MD: Naval Institute Press, 2018), p. 86.

20 This is not a new argument in Chinese circles, but it has only recently gained prominence in Western thinking. See Mitch Williamson, 'Strategic Geography of Chinese Sea Power II', Weapons and Warfare, 15 October 2020, https://weaponsandwarfare.com/2020/10/15/strategic-geography-of-chinese-sea-power-ii/.

21 Yoshihara and Holmes, *Red Star Over the Pacific*, pp. 86–7.

22 Asia Maritime Transparency Initiative, 'China Island Tracker', https://amti.csis.org/island-tracker/china/.

23 For a PRC report on the standard map, see Ma Zhenhuan, '2023 Edition of China Map Released', *China Daily*, 28 August 2023, https://www.chinadaily.com.cn/a/202308/28/WS64ec91c2a31035260b81ea5b.html. For an American report, see Jennifer Jett, 'China's New Map Outrages Its

Neighbors', NBC News, 1 September 2023, https://www.nbcnews.com/news/world/china-new-map-anger-india-south-china-sea-border-disputes-rcna102921.

24 Abe Shinzo, 'Asia's Democratic Security Diamond', Project Syndicate, 27 December 2012, https://www.project-syndicate.org/magazine/a-strategic-alliance-for-japan-and-india-by-shinzo-abe?barrier=accesspaylog.

25 Bilahari Kausikan, 'Navigating the New Era of Great-power Competition', *Foreign Affairs*, 11 April 2023, https://www.foreignaffairs.com/united-states/china-great-power-competition-russia-guide.

26 President of Russia, 'Joint Statement of the Russian Federation and the People's Republic of China on the International Relations Entering a New Era and the Global Sustainable Development'.

27 Kevin Rudd, *The Avoidable War: The Dangers of a Catastrophic Conflict between the US and Xi Jinping's China* (New York: Public Affairs, 2022).

28 See Rudd, *The Avoidable War*: in chapter 16 he writes that 'if the US declined to use nuclear weapons in Korea, Vietnam and the Taiwan Strait crises of the 1950s when there was negligible risk of any form of nuclear retaliation, the US would not do so over Taiwan in the 2020s, when the escalation risks are much greater'. Yet this is to compare apples with oranges: eschewing nuclear use in wars with non-nuclear powers is rather different from leaving nuclear weapons aside when in a major war with a superpower that is your rival for global leadership, and in which you clearly hold a strong nuclear advantage.

29 'A Conversation with Ambassador Kevin Rudd, Australia's New Ambassador to the United States', Centre for Strategic and International Studies, Washington DC, 6 June 2023, https://www.csis.org/analysis/conversation-ambassador-kevin-rudd-australias-new-ambassador-united-states.

30 Graham Allison, *Destined for War: Can America and China Escape Thucydides's Trap?* (Boston, MA: Houghton Mifflin Harcourt, 2017).

31 See, for example, Joseph S. Nye, Jr, 'Peak China?', Project Syndicate, 3 January 2023, https://www.project-syndicate.org/commentary/peak-china-debate-calls-for-careful-assessment-by-joseph-s-nye-2023-01.

Chapter Two

1 For the 2014 sanctions, see Anders Åslund, 'Western Economic Sanctions on Russia over Ukraine, 2014–2019', CESifo Forum, vol. 20, December 2019, https://www.cesifo.org/DocDL/CESifo-Forum-2019-4-aslund-economic-sanctions-december.pdf. For a preliminary assessment of the 2022 sanctions, see 'The Economic Impact of Russia Sanctions', Congressional Research Service, 13 December 2022, https://crsreports.congress.gov/product/pdf/IF/IF12092.

2 Guy Faulconbridge and Soo-Hyang Choi, 'Putin and North Korea's Kim

Discuss Military Matters, Ukraine War and Satellites', Reuters, 14 September 2023, https://www.reuters.com/world/nkoreas-kim-meets-putin-missiles-launched-pyongyang-2023-09-13/.

3   See Charlie Vest, Agatha Kratz and Reva Goujon, 'The Global Economic Disruptions from a Taiwan Conflict', Rhodium Group, 14 December 2022, https://rhg.com/research/taiwan-economic-disruptions/; and Jennifer Welch et al., 'Xi, Biden and the $10 Trillion Cost of War over Taiwan', Bloomberg, 9 January 2024, https://www.bloomberg.com/news/features/2024-01-09/if-china-invades-taiwan-it-would-cost-world-economy-10-trillion?leadSource=uverify%20wall.

4   See, most notably, President of Russia, 'On the Historical Unity of Russians and Ukrainians', 12 July 2021, http://en.kremlin.ru/events/president/news/66181.

5   Ian H. Robertson, 'The Danger that Lurks Inside Vladimir Putin's Brain', *Psychology Today*, 17 March 2014, https://www.psychologytoday.com/ie/blog/the-winner-effect/201403/the-danger-lurks-inside-vladimir-putins-brain.

6   See also Ian Robertson and his fellow neurologist Lord David Owen, 'Inside Putin's Mind: Absolute Power Has Blinded Russia's New Tsar', *Sunday Times*, 26 February 2022, https://www.thetimes.co.uk/article/inside-putins-mind-absolute-power-has-blinded-russias-new-tsar-q8gws3v5j.

7   'China's Xi Goes Full Stalin with Purge', Politico, 6 December 2023, https://www.politico.eu/article/chinas-paranoid-purge-xi-jinping-li-keqiang-qin-gang-li-shangfu/.

8   'Why the Man Who Planned the Attacks on Pearl Harbor Advised Against Them', PearlHarbor.org, 24 June 2016, https://pearlharbor.org/blog/man-who-planned-the-attacks/.

9   Sharon Braithwaite, 'Zelensky Refuses US Offer to Evacuate, Saying "I Need Ammunition, Not a Ride"',CNN, 26 February 2022, https://edition.cnn.com/2022/02/26/europe/ukraine-zelensky-evacuation-intl/index.html.

10 For a crisp analysis of the invasion and blockade options with a realistic sense of how actions by either China or the US could quickly escalate the conflict, see Brendan Taylor, *Dangerous Decade: Taiwan's Security and Crisis Management*, Adelphi 470 (Abingdon: Routledge for the IISS, 2019), pp. 108–13.

11 Republic of China (Taiwan), 'National Statistics: Total Population', https://eng.stat.gov.tw/Point.aspx?sid=t.9&n=4208&sms=11713.

12 See William S. Murray and Ian Easton, 'The Chinese Invasion Threat: Taiwan's Defense and American Strategy in Asia', *Naval War College Review*, vol. 72, no. 1, Winter 2019, https://digital-commons.usnwc.edu/cgi/viewcontent.cgi?article=7877&context=nwc-review.

13 One example of this term being used in this way can be found in 'Building Resilience for the Future: The Case of Ukraine', Swedish Civil Contingencies Agency, September 2023, https://www.msb.se/siteassets/dokument/publikationer/english-publications/building-resilience-for-the-future---lessons-from-ukraine.pdf.

Chapter Three

1. In *Deterrence* (Cambridge: Polity Press, 2004), Lawrence Freedman discusses how deterrence in the post-Cold War period was for a time superseded by the idea of pre-emption, in part because new adversaries such as al-Qaeda and the Islamic State (ISIS) were less susceptible to the threat of punishment or in any general sense to the idea of deterrence by denial. Michael J. Mazarr refocuses the concept on inter-state conflict while underlining the need for deterrence to be clearly directed at a specific objective. See Michael J. Mazarr, 'Understanding Deterrence', RAND Corporation, 19 April 2018, https://www.rand.org/pubs/perspectives/PE295.html.
2. Jim Garamone, US Department of Defense, 'Concept of Integrated Deterrence Will Be Key to National Defense Strategy, DOD Official Says', DOD News, 8 December 2021, https://www.defense.gov/News/News-Stories/Article/Article/2866963/concept-of-integrated-deterrence-will-be-key-to-national-defense-strategy-dod-o/h.
3. Freedman, *Deterrence*, p. 117.
4. Office of the Historian, US Department of State, 'Joint Statement Following Discussions with Leaders of the People's Republic of China', 27 February 1972, https://history.state.gov/historicaldocuments/frus1969-76v17/d203.

Chapter Four

1. John Lewis Gaddis, *The Long Peace: Inquiries Into the History of the Cold War* (New York: Oxford University Press, 1987).
2. Laura Alfaro and Davin Chor, 'Global Supply Chains: The Looming "Great Reallocation"', paper prepared for the Jackson Hole Symposium organised by the Federal Reserve Bank of Kansas City, 30 August 2023, https://www.kansascityfed.org/Jackson%20Hole/documents/9774/AlfaroChor_JacksonHole_30Aug2023.pdf.
3. Chris Miller, *Chip War: The Fight for the World's Most Critical Technology* (New York: Scribner, 2022).
4. Josh Rogin, *Chaos under Heaven: Trump, Xi, and the Battle for the Twenty-first Century* (New York: Houghton Mifflin Harcourt, 2021).
5. See also Bill Emmott, *Rivals: How the Power Struggle between China, India and Japan Will Shape Our Next Decade* (London: Allen Lane, 2008).
6. Private remarks to an unnamed senator, reported by Josh Rogin in *Chaos under Heaven*, p. 44.
7. Lauly Li and Cheng Ting-Fang, 'Pompeo Urges Washington to Recognize Taiwan as Sovereign Nation', Nikkei Asia, 4 March 2022, https://asia.nikkei.com/Politics/International-relations/Pompeo-urges-Washington-to-recognize-Taiwan-as-sovereign-nation.
8. Josh Boak, Aamer Madhani and Zeke Miller, 'Biden: US Would

Intervene with Military to Defend Taiwan', Associated Press, 23 May 2022, https://apnews.com/article/russia-ukraine-biden-taiwan-china-4fb0ad0567ed5bbe46c01dd758e6c62b.

9   Former president Donald Trump interviewed by Maria Bartiromo, *Sunday Morning Futures*, Fox News, 16 July 2023. This was also reported in Judy Lin and Bryan Chuang, 'Trump Accuses Taiwan of Taking Away America's Semiconductor Business', DigiTimes Asia, 18 July 2023, https://www.digitimes.com/news/a20230718PD207/ic-manufacturing-semiconductor-industry-us-taiwan-trade.html.

10 Office of the Historian, US Department of State, 'Joint Statement Following Discussions with Leaders of the People's Republic of China', 27 February 1972, https://history.state.gov/historicaldocuments/frus1969-76v17/d203.

11 For the number of service members in South Korea, see Jim Garamone, US Department of Defense, 'U.S., South Korea Want Peace in Indo-Pacific', DOD News, 31 January 2023, https://www.defense.gov/News/News-Stories/Article/Article/3282870/us-south-korea-want-peace-in-indo-pacific/#:~:text=There%20are%2028%2C500%20U.S.%20service,the%20Combined%20Forces%20—%20Korea.

12 For the debate, see, for example, Jean Mackenzie, 'Nuclear Weapons: Why South Koreans Want the Bomb', BBC News, 22 April 2023, https://www.bbc.com/news/world-asia-65333139. For an overview of South Korea's position, see Seukhoon Paul Choi, 'As World Order Shifts, So Does South Korean Security Policy', Arms Control Association, July/August 2023, https://www.armscontrol.org/act/2023-07/features/world-order-shifts-does-south-korean-security-policy.

13 This is based on IISS calculations. A carrier strike group on its own could sail at 30 knots, but if support ships are needed the best assumption is 20 knots. The Japanese port of Sasebo is nearer to Taiwan than Yokosuka is, but Yokosuka is cited because it is the main port from which a large naval force would probably depart.

14 Ministry of Foreign Affairs of Japan, 'United States–Japan Roadmap for Realignment Implementation', 1 May 2006, https://www.mofa.go.jp/region/n-america/us/security/scc/doc0605.html.

15 Maricar Cinco, '2024 Transfer of Okinawa-based Marines to Guam on Course: U.S. Marines', Kyodo News, 9 December 2022, https://english.kyodonews.net/news/2022/12/d96faaa52e79-2024-transfer-of-okinawa-based-marines-to-guam-on-course-us-marines.html; and IISS assessments.

16 US Marine Corps, 'Dynamic Force Employment', 2 August 2021, https://www.marines.mil/News/News-Display/Article/2708002/.

17 Dzirhan Mahadzir, 'New Marine Littoral Regiment Key to Expanded Pacific Security Cooperation, U.S., Japanese Leaders Say', USNI News, 12 January 2023, https://news.usni.org/2023/01/12/new-marine-littoral-regiment-key-to-expanded-pacific-security-cooperation-u-s-japanese-leaders-say.

18 *Ibid.*

19 Joseph Ditzler, '"Bittersweet": Air Force Begins Phased Withdrawal of F-15 Eagles from Okinawa',

Stars and Stripes, 2 December 2022, https://www.stripes.com/branches/air_force/2022-12-02/f15-eagles-phased-withdrawal-okinawa-8271510.html; and Matthew M. Burke and Keishi Koja, 'F-22 Raptors Begin Rotating into Okinawa to Replace Kadena's Aging F-15 Fleet', Stars and Stripes, 4 November 2022, https://www.stripes.com/branches/air_force/2022-11-04/air-force-raptors-f-15-kadena-okinawa-7923586.html.

[20] Seth Robson, 'Air Force Moving Reaper Squadron in Japan South to Okinawa', Stars and Stripes, 6 October 2023, https://www.stripes.com/branches/air_force/2023-10-06/reaper-drones-kyushu-okinawa-air-force-japan-11613613.html.

[21] Mallory Shelbourne, 'Navy Expanding Attack Submarine Presence on Guam as a Hedge against Growing Chinese Fleet', USNI News, 2 November 2022, https://news.usni.org/2022/11/02/navy-expanding-attack-submarine-presence-on-guam-as-a-hedge-against-growing-chinese-fleet. The *Los Angeles*-class nuclear-powered attack submarines (SSNs) are the generation that were built from 1972 to 1996, and are now being gradually replaced by the newer *Virginia* class.

[22] Australian Submarine Agency, 'Submarine Rotational Force–West', https://www.asa.gov.au/aukus/submarine-rotational-force-west#:~:text=From%20as%20early%20as%202027,West%20(SRF%2DWest).

[23] The INF treaty was originally signed in 1987 by the United States and the Soviet Union.

[24] Veerle Nouwens et al., 'Long-range Strike Capabilities in the Asia-Pacific: Implications for Regional Security', IISS, January 2024, https://www.iiss.org/globalassets/media-library---content--migration/files/research-papers/2024/01/iiss_long-range-strike-capabilities-in-the-asia-pacific_implications-for-regional-stability_012024.pdf.

[25] US Embassy in the Philippines, 'Enhanced Defense Cooperation Agreement (EDCA) Fact Sheet', 20 March 2023, https://ph.usembassy.gov/enhanced-defense-cooperation-agreement-edca-fact-sheet/.

[26] Government of Japan, Ministry of Defense, 'Defense Buildup Program', 16 December 2022, https://www.mod.go.jp/j/approach/agenda/guideline/plan/pdf/program_en.pdf.

[27] On the proportion of such chips produced in Taiwan, see Debby Wu, 'TSMC Facilities to Resume Production Overnight after Quake', Bloomberg, 3 April 2024, https://www.bloomberg.com/news/articles/2024-04-03/tsmc-evacuates-production-lines-after-major-taiwan-quake?embedded-checkout=true.

[28] For the texts of the US–China Communiqués of 1972, 1979 and 1982, see 'Taiwan: Texts of the Taiwan Relations Act, the U.S.–China Communiqués, and the "Six Assurances"', Congressional Research Service Report for Congress, 21 May 1998, https://www.everycrsreport.com/files/19980521_96-246F_a5b0e9334d4b4028eeb7dcb41626bddef3dc2c9a.pdf.

[29] For TSMC's investments in the US, see Natalie Sherman, 'TSMC Wins Subsidies to Expand US Chip Manufacturing in Arizona', BBC News, 8 April 2024, https://www.bbc.co.uk/news/business-68763232.

[30] *Ibid.*

[31] *Ibid.*

Chapter Five

1. See Ian Rowen, 'Inside Taiwan's Sunflower Movement: Twenty-four Days in a Student-occupied Parliament, and the Future of the Region', *Journal of Asian Studies*, vol. 74, no. 1, February 2015, https://www.cambridge.org/core/journals/journal-of-asian-studies/article/inside-taiwans-sunflower-movement-twentyfour-days-in-a-studentoccupied-parliament-and-the-future-of-the-region/DB4A7B57538A6F06DC6C8CF0058C8040.
2. *Ibid*.
3. Cheng Ting-Fang and Lauly Li, 'Taiwan Opposition Candidate Vows to Boost Defenses to Deter China', Nikkei Asia, 11 January 2024, https://asia.nikkei.com/Politics/Taiwan-elections/Taiwan-opposition-candidate-vows-to-boost-defenses-to-deter-China.
4. Election Study Center, National Chengchi University, 'Taiwan Independence vs. Unification with the Mainland (1994/12–2023/06)', 22 February 2024, https://esc.nccu.edu.tw/PageDoc/Detail?fid=7801&id=6963.
5. It is worth noting that the term used in Taiwan is generally 'unification' rather than 'reunification', signifying a lack of acceptance that Taiwan is part of China.
6. Republic of China (Taiwan), 'National Statistics: Total Population', https://eng.stat.gov.tw/Point.aspx?sid=t.9&n=4208&sms=11713.
7. Election Study Center, National Chengchi University, 'Taiwanese / Chinese Identity (1992/06–2023/12)', 22 February 2024, https://esc.nccu.edu.tw/PageDoc/Detail?fid=7800&id=6961.
8. IISS Military Balance+, https://milbalplus.iiss.org/. Many analysts believe China's official defence budget considerably understates its true spending: see, for example, Meia Nouwens and Lucie Béraud-Sudreau, 'Assessing Chinese Defence Spending: Proposals for New Methodologies', IISS Research Paper, 31 March 2020, https://www.iiss.org/research-paper/2020/03/assessing-chinese-defence-spending/.
9. Timothy R. Heath, Sale Lilly and Eugeniu Han, 'Can Taiwan Resist a Large-scale Military Attack by China?', RAND Corporation, 27 June 2023, https://www.rand.org/pubs/research_reports/RRA1658-1.html.
10. See William S. Murray and Ian Easton, 'The Chinese Invasion Threat: Taiwan's Defense and American Strategy in Asia', *Naval War College Review*, vol. 72, no. 1, Winter 2019, https://digital-commons.usnwc.edu/cgi/viewcontent.cgi?article=7877&context=nwc-review; and Ministry of National Defense, Republic of China, '2021 Quadrennial Defense Review', https://www.ustaiwandefense.com/tdnswp/wp-content/uploads/2021/03/2021-Taiwan-Quadrennial-Defense-Review-QDR.pdf.
11. Republic of China (Taiwan), 'National Statistics: Total Population'.
12. See Thompson Chau, 'Taiwan Submarine Dream Surfaces as China Tensions Rise', Nikkei Asia, 19 September 2023, https://asia.nikkei.com/Spotlight/Asia-Insight/Taiwan-submarine-dream-surfaces-as-China-tensions-rise#; and Thompson Chau, 'Taiwan Unveils "Narwhal", Its

First Home-built Submarine', Nikkei Asia, 28 September 2023, https://asia.nikkei.com/Politics/International-relations/Taiwan-tensions/Taiwan-unveils-Narwhal-its-first-home-built-submarine.

13 Gordon Arthur, 'Taiwan Begins Building Anti-submarine Frigate', Defense News, 23 January 2023, https://www.defensenews.com/naval/2024/01/23/taiwan-begins-building-anti-submarine-frigate/.

14 John Dotson, 'Taiwan's "Military Force Restructuring Plan" and the Extension of Conscripted Military Service', Global Taiwan Institute, 8 February 2023, https://globaltaiwan.org/2023/02/taiwan-military-force-restructuring-plan-and-the-extension-of-conscripted-military-service/.

15 IISS Military Balance+, https://milbalplus.iiss.org/.

16 Chen Yu-fu, 'Robert Tsao Pledges Money to Make 1m Combat Drones', *Taipei Times*, 24 September 2022, https://www.taipeitimes.com/News/taiwan/archives/2022/09/24/2003785860.

17 Hsu Tzu-ling and Jake Chung, 'DPP Lawmaker Urges Cyberdefense Priority', *Taipei Times*, 9 February 2024, https://www.taipeitimes.com/News/taiwan/archives/2024/02/09/2003813312.

18 See, for example, Helen Fitzwilliam, 'To Deter China, Taiwan Can Learn from Ukraine and Israel–Hamas War', Chatham House, 1 December 2023, https://www.chathamhouse.org/publications/the-world-today/2023-12/deter-china-taiwan-can-learn-ukraine-and-israel-hamas-war.

19 Doublethink Lab, https://doublethinklab.org. See also Doublethink's '2022 Taiwan Election: Foreign Influence Observation Report', 21 June 2023, https://medium.com/doublethinklab/2022-taiwan-election-foreign-influence-observation-report-89951af668f1.

20 Government of the Republic of China (Taiwan), Ministry of Economic Affairs, Energy Administration, 'What Is the Existing Energy Mix and Current Energy Policy in Taiwan?', 28 December 2023, https://www.moeaea.gov.tw/ECW/english/content/Content.aspx?menu_id=1679.

21 Joseph Webster, 'Does Taiwan's Massive Reliance on Energy Imports Put Its Security at Risk?', Atlantic Council, 7 July 2023, https://www.atlanticcouncil.org/blogs/new-atlanticist/does-taiwans-massive-reliance-on-energy-imports-put-its-security-at-risk/#:~:text=The%20island%20is%20highly%20dependent,comes%20from%20the%20Middle%20East.

22 Gavin Maguire, 'Taiwan Aims to Shed Dirty Power Reputation with Big Wind Push', Reuters, 28 September 2023, https://www.reuters.com/markets/commodities/taiwan-aims-shed-dirty-power-reputation-with-big-wind-push-maguire-2023-09-28/.

23 Government of the Republic of China (Taiwan), Ministry of Economic Affairs, Energy Administration, 'Management of Oil Security Stockpile', 21 February 2023, https://www.moeaea.gov.tw/ECW/english/content/Content.aspx?menu_id=8675.

24 IMF, 'Taiwan Province of China: Datasets', https://www.imf.org/external/datamapper/profile/TWN; and IMF, 'People's Republic of China: Datasets', https://www.imf.org/external/datamapper/profile/CHN.

25 Jeff Ferry, 'Currency Misalignment Monitor, June 2023', Coalition

for a Prosperous America, 1 June 2023, https://prosperousamerica. org/currency-misalignment-monitor/#:~:text=Taiwan%27s%20 currency%2C%20the%20Taiwanese%20 dollar,the%20most%20recent%20 currency%20moves. This calculation is based on a model showing what exchange-rate movements would be required to achieve zero current-account balances, which is arguably unrealistically stringent but nonetheless gives a broad assessment of the level of undervaluation.
26   Masahiro Okoshi, 'US Starts Pushing Taiwan to Address Undervalued Currency', Nikkei Asia, 17 April 2021, https://asia.nikkei.com/Business/ Markets/Currencies/US-starts-pushing-Taiwan-to-address-undervalued-currency.
27   The most recent switch of diplomatic recognition to the PRC was by the tiny island state of Nauru on 15 January 2024, just after Taiwan's elections. See Taijing Wu and Ken Moritsugu, 'Nauru Switches Diplomatic Recognition from Taiwan to China', Associated Press, 16 January 2024, https://apnews.com/article/taiwan-nauru-china-diplomacy-f8c6b74c03b61b51415c00b9e2bc32e1.
28   Government of the Republic of China (Taiwan), Ministry of Foreign Affairs, 'New Southbound Policy Portal', https://nspp.mofa.gov.tw/nsppe/.
29   Republic of China (Taiwan), Ministry of Finance, 'Annual External Trade Report in 2023', https://service.mof. gov.tw/public/Data/statistic/bulletin/ 112/2023%E8%8B%B1%E6%96%87%E 5%88%86%E6%9E%90.pdf.
30   Lin Tzu-yao and Cathy Fang, 'Lai Causes White House Debate', *Taipei Times*, 18 August 2023, https://www. taipeitimes.com/News/editorials/ archives/2023/08/18/2003804901.
31   Bonnie S. Glaser, Jessica Chen Weiss and Thomas J. Christensen, 'Taiwan and the True Sources of Deterrence', *Foreign Affairs*, January/February 2024, https://www.foreignaffairs.com/taiwan/ taiwan-china-true-sources-deterrence.

Chapter Six

1   Simina Mistreanu, 'China Releases TV Documentary Showcasing Army's Ability to Attack Taiwan', Associated Press, 7 August 2023, https://apnews. com/article/china-taiwan-documentary-attack-invasion-chasing-dreams-4105d5f0bde59337d90f1e67d149b32c; and 'CCTV Reveals Unprecedented Footage of Shandong Aircraft Carrier in Taiwan Strait amid Rising Tensions', China Arms, 2 August 2023, https:// www.china-arms.com/2023/08/ unprecedented-footage-of-shandong-aircraft-carrier-in-taiwan-strait/.
2   US Department of Defense, 'Military and Security Developments Involving the People's Republic of China: Annual Report to Congress 2023', https://media.defense.gov/2023/ Oct/19/2003323409/-1/-1/1/2023-MILITARY-AND-SECURITY-DEVELOPMENTS-INVOLVING-THE-PEOPLES-REPUBLIC-OF-CHINA.PDF. This is often referred to as the 'China Military Power Report'.
3   See Richard C. Bush, 'Taiwan Should Exercise Restraint in Reacting to China's Anti-Secession Law', Brookings

Institution, 24 March 2005, https://www.brookings.edu/articles/taiwan-should-exercise-restraint-in-reacting-to-the-challenge-of-chinas-anti-secession-law/. For the Republic of China's official response, see Republic of China (Taiwan), Mainland Affairs Council, 'The Official Position of the Republic of China (Taiwan) on the People's Republic of China's Anti-Secession Law', 29 March 2005, https://www.mac.gov.tw/en/News_Content.aspx?n=8A319E37A32E01EA&sms=2413CFE1BCE87E0E&s=D1B0D66D5788F2DE.

4   For a review of Chinese war plans, capabilities and scenarios, see William S. Murray and Ian Easton, 'The Chinese Invasion Threat: Taiwan's Defense and American Strategy in Asia', *Naval War College Review*, vol. 72, no. 1, Winter 2019, https://digital-commons.usnwc.edu/cgi/viewcontent.cgi?article=7877&context=nwc-review.

5   'China Releases White Paper on Taiwan Question, Reunification in New Era', Xinhua, 10 August 2022, https://english.www.gov.cn/archive/whitepaper/202208/10/content_WS62f34f46c6d02e533532f0ac.html.

6   Cherry Hitkari, 'China's Taiwan Policy in the "New Era"', Lowy Institute, 16 August 2022, https://www.lowyinstitute.org/the-interpreter/china-s-taiwan-policy-new-era.

7   See, for example, Mark F. Cancian, Matthew Cancian and Eric Heginbotham, 'The First Battle of the Next War: Wargaming a Chinese Invasion of Taiwan', Center for Strategic and International Studies, 9 January 2023, https://www.csis.org/analysis/first-battle-next-war-wargaming-chinese-invasion-taiwan.

8   For how the PLA Rocket Force would find it considerably harder to hit an intervention force – multiple moving targets – than fixed bases, see Veerle Nouwens et al., 'Long-range Strike Capabilities in the Asia-Pacific', IISS, January 2024, https://www.iiss.org/research-paper/2024/01/long-range-strike-capabilities-in-the--asia-pacific-implications-for-regional-stability/.

9   Henry Boyd, Meia Nouwens and Veerle Nouwens, 'PLA Sharpens Nuclear and Conventional Capabilities but Still Has Work to Do, US Says', IISS Military Balance blog, 1 November 2023, https://www.iiss.org/online-analysis/military-balance/2023/10/pla-sharpens-nuclear-and-conventional-capabilities-but-still-has-work-to-do-us-says/.

10 US Department of Defense, 'Military and Security Developments Involving the People's Republic of China: Annual Report to Congress 2023'.

11 David Vergun, US Department of Defense, 'Russia Reportedly Supplying Enriched Uranium to China', DOD News, 8 March 2023, https://www.defense.gov/News/News-Stories/Article/Article/3323381/russia-reportedly-supplying-enriched-uranium-to-china/.

12 Fiona S. Cunningham, 'The Unknowns about China's Nuclear Modernization Program', Arms Control Association, June 2023, https://www.armscontrol.org/act/2023-06/features/unknowns-about-chinas-nuclear-modernization-program.

13 Roy D. Kamphausen (ed.), *Modernizing Deterrence: How China Coerces, Compels, and Deters* (Seattle, WA: National Bureau of Asian Research, 2023), https://www.nbr.org/wp-content/uploads/pdfs/publications/modernizing-deterrence_feb2023.pdf.

14 Brandon J. Babin, 'Xi Jinping's Strangelove: The Need for a

Deterrence-based Offset Strategy', in Kamphausen (ed.), *Modernizing Deterrence*, p. 82.

15 *Ibid.*, p. 81.

16 Stuart Lau, 'China's Xi Warns Putin Not to Use Nuclear Arms in Ukraine', Politico, 4 November 2022, https://www.politico.eu/article/china-xi-jinping-warns-vladimir-putin-not-to-use-nuclear-arms-in-ukraine-olaf-scholz-germany-peace-talks/.

17 Private remarks to an unnamed senator, reported by Josh Rogin in *Chaos under Heaven: Trump, Xi, and the Battle for the Twenty-first Century* (New York: Houghton Mifflin Harcourt, 2021), p. 44.

18 See, for example, Jennifer Lind, 'South China Sea as a Chinese Lake', *New York Times*, 23 August 2016, https://www.nytimes.com/roomfordebate/2016/08/23/is-playing-tough-in-chinas-interest/south-china-sea-as-a-chinese-lake.

19 'Rising International Support for Taiwan', IISS *Strategic Comments*, vol. 27, no. 35, December 2021.

20 Rupert Wingfield-Hayes, 'The US Is Quietly Arming Taiwan to the Teeth', BBC News, 6 November 2023, https://www.bbc.com/news/world-asia-67282107.

21 On international judicial rulings, see notably the 2016 ruling by the Permanent Court of Arbitration on a dispute brought by the Philippines – see Euan Graham, 'The Hague Tribunal's South China Sea Ruling: Empty Provocation or Slow-burning Influence?', Council of Councils, 18 August 2016, https://www.cfr.org/councilofcouncils/global-memos/hague-tribunals-south-china-sea-ruling-empty-provocation-or-slow-burning-influence. On a maritime code of conduct, see Prashanth Parameswaran, 'What's Behind the New China–ASEAN South China Sea Code of Conduct Talk Guidelines?', Asia Dispatches blog, Wilson Centre, 25 July 2023, https://www.wilsoncenter.org/blog-post/whats-behind-new-china-asean-south-china-sea-code-conduct-talk-guidelines.

Chapter Seven

1 C. Todd Lopez, US Department of Defense, 'Defense Secretary Says "Integrated Deterrence" Is Cornerstone of US Defense', DOD News, 30 April 2021, https://www.defense.gov/News/News-Stories/Article/Article/2592149/defense-secretary-says-integrated-deterrence-is-cornerstone-of-us-defense/.

2 Center for Strategic and International Studies (CSIS) Asia Maritime Transparency Initiative, 'More than Meets the Eye: Philippine Upgrades at EDCA Sites', 12 October 2023, https://amti.csis.org/more-than-meets-the-eye-philippine-upgrades-at-edca-sites/.

3 Demetri Sevastopulo and Kana Inagaki, 'US and Japan Announce "Most Significant" Upgrade to Military Alliance', *Financial Times*, 10 April 2024, https://on.ft.com/49Dv4wa.

4 Motoko Rich and Choe Sang-Hun, 'Japan and South Korea Make Nice, But Can It Last?', *New York Times*, 17 March 2023, https://www.nytimes.

com/2023/03/17/world/asia/japn-south-korea-relations.html.

5   Republic of Korea, Ministry of Foreign Affairs, 'Strategy for a Free, Peaceful, and Prosperous Indo-Pacific Region', 28 December 2022, https://www.mofa.go.kr/eng/brd/m_5676/view.do?seq=322133.

6   IISS Military Balance+. In 2023, Japan's defence budget of US$48.6 billion was the world's ninth largest at market exchange rates. Where Japan's defence budget will rank in 2027 depends firstly on what happens to the currently historically weak yen exchange rate, which depressed the 2023 ranking despite a substantial spending rise in yen terms, but secondly on how defence spending develops in Russia, where total military expenditure reached an estimated US$109bn in 2023, placing it third place behind the US and China. Next come India, the UK, Saudi Arabia, Germany and France.

7   'Japan's New National-security and Defence Strategies', IISS *Strategic Comments*, vol. 29, no. 1, January 2023, https://www.iiss.org/publications/strategic-comments/2023/japans-new-national-security-and-defence-strategies/.

8   The Global Combat Air Programme, to be led by BAE Systems in the UK, Leonardo in Italy and Mitsubishi Heavy Industries in Japan. See BAE Systems, 'Global Combat Air Programme', https://www.baesystems.com/en/product/global-combat-air-programme.

9   Apparently Nakasone did not actually say this, but the quote entered circulation thanks to an imaginative official translator. See Don Oberdorfer, 'How to Make a Japanese Brouhaha', *Washington Post*, 19 March 1983, https://www.washingtonpost.com/archive/opinions/1983/03/20/how-to-make-a-japanese-brouhaha/0e508dd9-105b-4673-98aa-1e63fe8eae08/.

10   The Royal Navy operates two aircraft carriers, the French Navy just one.

11   Government of Japan, Ministry of Defense, 'Defense of Japan 2023', https://www.mod.go.jp/en/publ/w_paper/wp2023/DOJ2023_EN_Full.pdf.

12   Yusuke Takeuchi, 'Japan's Fighter-jet Export Plans Hit Snag as Komeito Backtracks', Nikkei Asia, 7 December 2023, https://asia.nikkei.com/Business/Aerospace-Defense-Industries/Japan-s-fighter-jet-export-plans-hit-snag-as-Komeito-backtracks#.

13   'Japan Eases Weapons Export Rules to Sell Fighter Jets Abroad', Nikkei Asia, 26 March 2024, https://asia.nikkei.com/Politics/Defense/Japan-eases-weapons-export-rules-to-sell-fighter-jets-abroad.

14   The next general election for the lower house of the Diet, the House of Representatives, is due to take place by October 2025 at the latest, although the prime minister can call an election at any time. The less powerful upper house, the House of Councillors, is also due to have an election in 2025.

15   Prime Minister of Japan and His Cabinet, 'The Constitution of Japan', https://japan.kantei.go.jp/constitution_and_government_of_japan/constitution_e.html.

16   *Ibid.*

17   Malcolm Cook, 'Despite Protests, Collective Self-defence and Abe Remain', The Interpreter, The Lowy Institute, 3 September 2015, https://www.lowyinstitute.org/the-interpreter/despite-protests-collective-self-defence-abe-remain.

18 See Ministry of Foreign Affairs of Japan, 'History of Japanese Peacekeeping Operations', https://www.mofa.go.jp/policy/un/pko/pdfs/contribution.pdf.

19 See Taizo Teramoto, 'Survey: 52% Say Constitution Is "Good", 37% Want Article 9 Changed', *Asahi Shimbun*, 3 May 2023, https://www.asahi.com/ajw/articles/14899830; and 'Yomiuri Poll: 61% Support Constitutional Revision', Japan News, 3 May 2023, https://japannews.yomiuri.co.jp/politics/politics-government/20230503-107407/.

20 In April 2021, prime minister Suga Yoshihide allowed Taiwan to be mentioned in a US–Japan communiqué for the first time in five decades. See Andrew Sharp, 'China Hits Back at Japan–US Statement that Names Taiwan', Nikkei Asia, 17 April 2021, https://asia.nikkei.com/Politics/International-relations/Biden-s-Asia-policy/China-hits-back-at-Japan-US-statement-that-names-Taiwan. Then, in June 2021, then-defense minister Kishi Nobuo stated that 'the peace and stability of Taiwan is directly connected to Japan'. See 'Tokyo Says Taiwan Security Directly Connected to Japan – Bloomberg', Reuters, 25 June 2021, https://www.reuters.com/article/idUSL3N2O64E5/.

21 Zuzanna Gwadera, 'US Approves the Sale of *Tomahawk* Cruise Missiles to Japan', IISS Missile Dialogue Initiative, 7 December 2023, https://www.iiss.org/online-analysis/missile-dialogue-initiative/2023/12/us-approves-the-sale-of-tomahawk-cruise-missiles-to-japan/.

22 For a history of Japan's intelligence efforts, see Richard J Samuels, *Special Duty: A History of the Japanese Intelligence Community* (Ithaca, NY: Cornell University Press, 2019); and 'Cybersecurity Laws and Regulations Japan 2024', ICLG.com, 14 November 2023, https://iclg.com/practice-areas/cybersecurity-laws-and-regulations/japan.

23 In English, the name Ryukyu is often used for the whole chain of islands from south of Kyushu to Yonaguni, but in Japanese the word Ryukyu applies just to the smaller group of islands (including Okinawa) that belonged to the Ryukyu Kingdom from 1429 to 1879. The Ryukyu Kingdom was considered by China to be a tributary state during the Ming Dynasty (1368–1644), which sometimes provides the basis for claims by Chinese scholars that Okinawa and the other Ryukyu Islands should really belong to China. Nansei-shoto (southwest arc) is the official Japanese name for the whole chain.

24 William Gallo, 'Taiwan Tensions Fuel Anxiety on Japan's Tiny Yonaguni Island', Voice of America, 24 March 2023, https://www.voanews.com/a/taiwan-tensions-fuel-anxiety-on-japan-s-tiny-yonaguni-island-/7019581.html.

25 Ministry of Foreign Affairs of Japan, 'The Senkaku Islands', https://www.mofa.go.jp/region/asia-paci/senkaku/pdfs/senkaku_pamphlet.pdf.

26 See Michael J. Green, *Line of Advantage: Japan's Grand Strategy in the Era of Abe Shinzo* (New York: Columbia University Press, 2022).

27 Ken Moriyasu, 'Biden and Kishida Strengthen Bonds to Defend Global Order', Nikkei Asia, 10 April 2024, https://asia.nikkei.com/Politics/International-relations/Biden-and-

Kishida-strengthen-bonds-to-defend-global-order.
28   IMF, 'Japan: Datasets', https://www.imf.org/external/datamapper/profile/JPN.
29   Ministry of Foreign Affairs of Japan, 'Japan's Security Policy: Official Security Assistance (OSA)', 23 February 2024, https://www.mofa.go.jp/fp/ipc/page4e_001366.html.

Chapter Eight

1 US Department of State, Office of the Historian, 'The Australia, New Zealand and United States Security Treaty (ANZUS Treaty), 1951', https://history.state.gov/milestones/1945-1952/anzus.
2 US Department of State, 'U.S. Security Cooperation with Thailand: Fact Sheet', 31 October 2022, https://www.state.gov/u-s-security-cooperation-with-thailand/.
3 Center for Strategic and International Studies (CSIS) Asia Maritime Transparency Initiative, 'More than Meets the Eye: Philippine Upgrades at EDCA Sites', 12 October 2023, https://amti.csis.org/more-than-meets-the-eye-philippine-upgrades-at-edca-sites/.
4 US Department of Defense, 'Fact Sheet: US–Philippines Bilateral Defense Guidelines', 3 May 2023, https://www.defense.gov/News/Releases/Release/Article/3383607/fact-sheet-us-philippines-bilateral-defense-guidelines/.
5 Gregory B. Poling, 'The Transformation of the US–Philippines Alliance', CSIS, 2 February 2023, https://www.csis.org/analysis/transformation-us-philippines-alliance.
6 Euan Graham, 'The Hague Tribunal's South China Sea Ruling: Empty Provocation or Slow-burning Influence?', Council of Councils, 18 August 2016, https://www.cfr.org/councilofcouncils/global-memos/hague-tribunals-south-china-sea-ruling-empty-provocation-or-slow-burning-influence. The court ruled that China's 'nine-dash line' claim over the South China Sea had no legal foundation.
7 George Wright, 'South China Sea: Philippine and Chinese Vessels Collide in Contested Waters', BBC News, 10 December 2023, https://www.bbc.com/news/world-asia-67668930.
8 Confidential interview with a senior Philippines defence official, June 2023.
9 IISS, Military Balance+, https://milbalplus.iiss.org/.
10 Ministry of Foreign Affairs of Japan, 'Japan's Security Policy: Official Security Assistance (OSA)', 23 February 2024, https://www.mofa.go.jp/fp/ipc/page4e_001366.html.
11 Nadeem Badshah, 'France's Outgoing Foreign Minister Welcomes Defeat of Scott Morrison', *Guardian*, 21 May 2022, https://www.theguardian.com/world/2022/may/21/frances-outgoing-foreign-minister-welcomes-defeat-of-scott-morrison.
12 For an authoritative analysis of the AUKUS deal, see Nick Childs, 'The AUKUS Anvil: Promise and Peril', *Survival: Global Politics and Strategy*, vol. 65, no. 5, October–November 2023, https://www.iiss.org/online-

analysis/survival-online/2023/10/the-aukus-anvil-promise-and-peril/, pp. 7–24.

13 'Australia Announces Compensation Deal with France for Scrapped Submarine Contract', France 24, 11 June 2022, https://www.france24.com/en/asia-pacific/20220611-australia-announces-compensation-deal-with-france-over-scrapped-submarine-contract.

14 Government of Australia, Department of Defence, '2020 Defence Strategic Update', 1 July 2020, https://www.defence.gov.au/about/strategic-planning/2020-defence-strategic-update.

15 Elbridge Colby of the Marathon Initiative, who worked at the Pentagon during the Trump administration, has been particularly vocal about this, albeit as part of a campaign to persuade both major US parties to invest more in building up the US defence-industrial base. See Elbridge Colby, 'AUKUS Going to "Face Challenges" and Is "At Risk of Falling Apart"', The Marathon Initiative, 3 November 2023, https://www.themarathoninitiative.org/2023/11/aukus-going-to-face-challenges-and-is-at-risk-of-falling-apart/; and 'VIDEO: Trump's Former Defence Advisor Slams "Crazy" AUKUS Submarine Deal', ABC News, 2 January 2024, https://www.abc.net.au/news/2024-01-03/trumps-former-defence-advisor-slams-crazy-aukus-sub-deal/103280982.

16 Childs, 'The AUKUS Anvil: Promise and Peril'.

17 IISS, *The Military Balance 2024* (Abingdon: Routledge for the IISS, 2024); 1st Lt Colin Kennard, 'U.S. Marines Reach 2,500 in Darwin for First Time', US Indo-Pacific Command, 26 July 2019, https://www.pacom.mil/Media/News/News-Article-View/Article/1918439/us-marines-reach-2500-in-darwin-for-first-time/; and Government of Australia, Department of Defence, 'Australia Welcomes United States Marines Back to Darwin', 22 March 2023, https://www.minister.defence.gov.au/media-releases/2023-03-22/australia-welcomes-united-states-marines-back-darwin.

18 Government of Australia, Submarine Agency, 'Submarine Rotational Force–West', https://www.asa.gov.au/aukus/submarine-rotational-force-west.

19 The Labor prime minister most closely identified with Australia's relatively pro-China period was Paul Keating (1991–96), who remains a vocal critic of his Labor successor, Prime Minister Anthony Albanese, and of the AUKUS deal. In 2021 he described Taiwan as being 'not a vital Australian interest'. See Helen Davidson and Daniel Hurst, 'Taiwan Hits Back after Paul Keating Says Its Status "Not a Vital Australian Interest"', *Guardian*, 10 November 2021, https://www.theguardian.com/australia-news/2021/nov/11/taiwan-hits-back-after-paul-keating-says-its-status-not-a-vital-australian-interest.

20 'Australia Has Faced Down China's Trade Bans and Emerged Stronger', *The Economist*, 23 May 2023, https://www.economist.com/asia/2023/05/23/australia-has-faced-down-chinas-trade-bans-and-emerged-stronger.

21 Anthony Albanese, '20th Asia Security Summit: The Shangri-La Dialogue, Keynote Address', IISS, 2 June 2023, https://www.iiss.

22. For the Comprehensive Strategic Partnership with Vietnam, see The White House, 'Joint Leaders' Statement: Elevating United States–Vietnam Relations to a Comprehensive Strategic Partnership', 11 September 2023, https://www.whitehouse.gov/briefing-room/statements-releases/2023/09/11/joint-leaders-statement-elevating-united-states-vietnam-relations-to-a-comprehensive-strategic-partnership/; for military exercises with Indonesia, see Fadlan Syam and Niniek Karmini, 'Australian and Indonesian Forces Deploy Battle Tanks in US-led Combat Drills amid Chinese Concern', Associated Press, 12 September 2023, https://apnews.com/article/indonesia-us-australia-garuda-shield-military-exercise-6db9f940f6f43e70cac974f41e289706#; and for the US–Singapore partnership, see Lynn Kuok, 'The U.S.–Singapore Partnership: A Critical Element of U.S. Engagement and Stability in the Asia-Pacific', Brookings Institution, 13 July 2026, https://www.brookings.edu/wp-content/uploads/2016/11/fp_20160713_singapore_partnership.pdf.

23. Henry Boyd et al., 'Taiwan, Cross-strait Stability and European Security: Implications and Response Options', IISS Research Paper, March 2022, https://www.iiss.org/en/research-paper/2022/03/taiwan-cross-strait-stability-and-european-security/.

24. In January 2024 South Korean police charged two engineers at a South Korean marine consultancy, SI Innotec, with illegally transferring submarine blueprints to Taiwan. See Christian Davies and Song Jung-a, 'South Koreans Charged with Leaking Submarine Secrets to Taiwan', *Financial Times*, 5 January 2024, https://www.ft.com/content/e33fe697-1e12-4214-9c45-8e677a1e61d8.

25. United Nations Population Fund, 'World Population Dashboard: Indonesia', https://www.unfpa.org/data/world-population/ID.

26. The largest is Vietnam, with 450,000 in active service. See IISS, Military Balance+.

27. IISS, *The Military Balance 2024*. Singapore's GDP per capita in 2023 ranked it sixth in the world according to IMF data. Among other ASEAN members only the tiny oil state of Brunei comes close at number 27, followed far behind by Malaysia (67), Indonesia (114), Vietnam (120), the Philippines (132), Laos (150), Cambodia (152) and Myanmar (168). See IMF, 'GDP per Capita, Current Prices', https://www.imf.org/external/datamapper/NGDPDPC@WEO/OEMDC/ADVEC/WEOWORLD.

28. IISS, Military Balance+.

29. Ian Storey, 'China's Missteps in Southeast Asia: Less Charm, More Offensive', The Jamestown Foundation China Brief, 17 December 2010, https://jamestown.org/program/chinas-missteps-in-southeast-asia-less-charm-more-offensive/.

30. For the reclaiming of land, see CSIS Asia Maritime Transparency Initiative, 'China Island Tracker', https://amti.csis.org/island-tracker/china/; for the nine-dash line, see 'How the "Nine-dash Line"

Fuels Tensions in the South China Sea', *The Economist*, https://www.economist.com/the-economist-explains/2023/02/10/how-the-nine-dash-line-fuels-tensions-in-the-south-china-sea.

31 The Permanent Court of Arbitration's ruling can be found here: 'The South China Sea Arbitration (The Republic of Philippines v. The People's Republic of China)', Permanent Court of Arbitration, https://pca-cpa.org/en/cases/7/. The CSIS Asia Maritime Transparency Initiative has monitored China's non-compliance with the ruling. See 'Failing or Incomplete? Grading the South China Sea Arbitration', CSIS Asia Maritime Transparency Initiative, 11 July 2019, https://amti.csis.org/failing-or-incomplete-grading-the-south-china-sea-arbitration/.

32 In the 2002 Declaration on the Conduct of Parties in the South China Sea, which was reaffirmed between ASEAN and China in 2012, the parties agreed to resolve territorial disputes in accordance with the 1982 UN Convention on the Law of the Sea, an undertaking that China ignored in 2016 when the Philippines brought its case under that very law. See ASEAN, 'Declaration on the Conduct of Parties in the South China Sea', 14 May 2012, https://asean.org/declaration-on-the-conduct-of-parties-in-the-south-china-sea-2/. For the new 'guidelines', see Prashanth Parameswaran, 'What's Behind the New China–ASEAN South China Sea Code of Conduct Talk Guidelines?', Wilson Center, 25 July 2023, https://www.wilsoncenter.org/blog-post/whats-behind-new-china-asean-south-china-sea-code-conduct-talk-guidelines.

33 ASEAN, 'The ASEAN Charter', ASEAN Secretariat, January 2008, https://asean.org/wp-content/uploads/images/archive/publications/ASEAN-Charter.pdf.

34 ASEAN, 'ASEAN Outlook on the Indo-Pacific', 23 July 2019, https://asean.org/asean2020/wp-content/uploads/2021/01/ASEAN-Outlook-on-the-Indo-Pacific_FINAL_22062019.pdf.

35 Benny Teh, 'What ASEAN Centrality?', The ASEAN Post, 1 January 2022, https://theaseanpost.com/article/what-asean-centrality.

36 'Malaysia Calls for "Strong" Measures on Myanmar as ASEAN Meets', Al-Jazeera, 5 September 2023, https://www.aljazeera.com/news/2023/9/5/malaysia-calls-for-strong-measures-on-myanmar-as-asean-meets.

37 ASEAN's founding fathers were Indonesia, Malaysia, the Philippines, Singapore and Thailand. Brunei was admitted in 1984, Vietnam in 1995, Laos and Myanmar in 1997 and Cambodia in 1999. See ASEAN, 'The Founding of ASEAN', https://asean.org/the-founding-of-asean/. For Kishore Mahbubani quote, see Kishore Mahbubani, 'Asia's Third Way', *Foreign Affairs*, 28 February 2023, https://www.foreignaffairs.com/southeast-asia/asias-third-way-asean-amid-great-power-competition. Note that although *Foreign Affairs* gave his article a headline implying this was covering the whole of Asia, in fact Ambassador Mahbubani's 'third way' does not encompass most of Asia but just ten of its countries.

38 See ASEAN, 'The Regional Comprehensive Economic Partnership (RCEP)', https://asean.org/our-communities/economic-community/

39 Richard Heydarian, 'ASEAN Members Are Finding Ways Around Bloc Paralysis', Nikkei Asia, 20 February 2024, https://asia.nikkei.com/Opinion/ASEAN-members-are-finding-ways-around-bloc-paralysis.
40 At market exchange rates.
41 IMF, 'GDP, current prices', https://www.imf.org/external/datamapper/NGDPD@WEO/OEMDC/ADVEC/WEOWORLD.

Conclusion

1. See John Lewis Gaddis, *The Cold War* (London: Penguin, 2005).
2. Lawrence Freedman, *Deterrence* (Cambridge: Polity Press, 2004).
3. See Iskander Rehman, *Planning for Protraction: A Historically Informed Approach to Great-power War and Sino-US Competition*, Adelphi 496–497 (Abingdon: Routledge for the IISS, 2023).
4. Gaddis, *The Cold War*, p. 262.
5. Some examples of work considering these various aspects of strengthening strategic stability, including its political and diplomatic elements, include Michael J. Mazarr et al., 'Stabilizing Great-power Rivalries', RAND, 29 November 2021, https://www.rand.org/pubs/research_reports/RRA456-1.html; 'China's Emergence as a Second Nuclear Peer: Implications for US Nuclear Deterrence Strategy', Center for Global Security Research at Lawrence Livermore National Laboratory, Spring 2023, https://cgsr.llnl.gov/content/assets/docs/CGSR_Two_Peer_230314.pdf; Ankit Panda, 'Indo-Pacific Missile Arsenals: Avoiding Spirals and Mitigating Escalation Risks', Carnegie Endowment for International Peace, 31 October 2023, https://carnegieendowment.org/2023/10/31/indo-pacific-missile-arsenals-avoiding-spirals-and-mitigating-escalation-risks-pub-90772; and William Leben, 'Escalation Risks in the Indo-Pacific: A Review for Practitioners', Australian Strategic Policy Institute, 23 February 2024, https://ad-aspi.s3.ap-southeast-2.amazonaws.com/2024-02/SR201%20Escalation%20risks%20in%20the%20Indo-Pacific.pdf?VersionId=Ec1JMi.G8DGKlGvD_w6Qf3B.rEYCW393.
6. Chelsey Wiley and William Alberque, 'Meagre Results from the US–China Meeting on Arms Control', IISS Missile Dialogue Initiative, 21 November 2023, https://www.iiss.org/online-analysis/missile-dialogue-initiative/2023/10/meagre-results-from-the-us-china-meeting-on-arms-control/.
7. Fiona S. Cunningham, 'The Unknowns about China's Nuclear Modernization Program', Arms Control Association, June 2023, https://www.armscontrol.org/act/2023-06/features/unknowns-about-chinas-nuclear-modernization-program.

INDEX

A

Abe Shinzo 31, 61–62, 120, 122, 127
Africa 33, 53
Air Defence Identification Zone 15, 24, 102
Albanese, Anthony 138, 141
Aquino, Noynoy 135
arms control 16, 20, 159, 160, 161
Association of Southeast Asian Nations (ASEAN) 31, 135, *145*, 146, 147, 148
AUKUS 70, 116, 138, 139, 140
Australia 15, 49, 57, 62, 66, 68, 70, 71, 94, 113, 116, 131, 134, 138
  Defence Strategic Update 138
  trade with China 141

B

Babin, Brandon J. 109
Baltic states 43
Biden, Joe 21, 22, 23, 42, 60, 62, 63, 86, 87, 100, 105, 112, 116, 129, 161
Bulletin of the Atomic Scientists 19, 20
  Doomsday Clock 19, 20
Bush, George W. 62

C

Campbell, Kurt 61
CCTV (Chinese state broadcaster) 99
Chen Shui-bian 96
Chiang Ching-kuo 26
Chiang Kai-shek 26, 31, 79, 146
China
  and Russia 11, 53, 57
  and US 13, 20, 21, 49, 74, 110, 133, 154
  anti-access/area denial (A2/AD) 67, 68, 70, 90, 104, 105
  Anti-Secession Law 100
  defence budget 150
  economy 150, 157
  Encyclopedia of China's Strategic Missile Force 109
  Joint Statement with Russia 11, 22, 33, 37
  nuclear weapons 49, 106, 110
  People's Liberation Army (PLA) 28, 29, 86, 89, *89,* 99, 100, 124
  People's Liberation Army Navy 140, 146
  standard map 31, *32*
China derangement syndrome 60
China Military Power Report 106

Note: Page numbers are italicised where terms appear in figures or maps.

Chinese Civil War 26
climate 17, 19
Clinton, Bill 22
Coalition for a Prosperous America 94
Cold War 9, 33, 34, 43, 49, 51, 52, 54, 58, 59, 63, 153, 156, 159
  negotiations 13, 14
  political and strategic consistency 16
commodities 38, 141
Comprehensive and Progressive Agreement for Trans-Pacific Partnership (CPTPP) 132, 143
Conventional Prompt Strike (CPS) 71
coronavirus 20, 141
counter-intervention 104
COVID-19 *see* coronavirus
Crimea 10, 37, 47, 79, 96
Cross-Strait Services Trade Agreement (CSSTA) 79, 80, 81
Cuban Missile Crisis 33, 51, 64, 154, 159
currencies *see* New Taiwan Dollar
cyber operations 106, 116, 125

D

Dark Eagle weapon 71
Davidson, Admiral Philip 25
Defense Advanced Research Projects Agency (DARPA) 130
Democratic Party of Japan 120
Democratic Progressive Party (DPP) 80, 82, 84, 87, 90, 94, 102
Deng Xiaoping 24
dictatorial regimes 40, 41, 154, 156
diplomacy 14
disinformation *see* narrative about strategy
Duterte, Rodrigo 135, 137

E

East Asia 12, *29*, 47, 53
East China Sea 28, 31, 47, 70, 73, 110, 111, 118, 142

Economic Cooperation Framework Agreement 80
elections 81, 82, 84, 88, 90, 95, 97, 117, 120
energy supplies 38, 93, 94
Enhanced Defense Cooperation Agreement (EDCA) 71, 116, 136, 138
escalation dominance 43, 49
Europe 11, 12, 36, 44, 53, 54, 74, 117, 142, 144, 148
extended deterrence 66

F

F-15 *Eagle* aircraft 69
F-22 *Raptor* aircraft 69
first island chain 28, *29*, 69
Five Eyes network 134
Foreign Military Financing (US) 112
France 117, 119, 138, 143
Free and Open Indo-Pacific (FOIP) 31

G

Gaddis, John Lewis 59, 158
Germany 142
great powers 28, 33, 34, 52
grey zone 85, 88, 101
Guam 30, 68, 70, 71, 72, 86, 104, 140, 154

H

Hamada Yasukazu 119
Hawaii 68, 72, 154
Hong Kong 79, 92, 95, 102, 103, 141
hotline between China and Taiwan 24
Hou You-ih 82
Hypersonic Attack Cruise Missiles 71

I

India *32*, 61, 62, 116, 144, 149
Indonesia 142, 144, 147, 149, 150

integrated deterrence 15, 52, 106, 116
Intermediate-Range Nuclear Forces
     Treaty 70

J

Japan 27, 31, 49, 53, 54, 57
  constitution 121–126, 131
  defence industry 118, 120, 121, 130
  defence spending 61, 86, 117, 118, 119, *128*, 130
  Defense Buildup Program 71, 118, 124, 125, 126
  intelligence agency 116, 117, 125, 129
  Japan Maritime Self-Defense Force (JMSDF) 67, 69, 119, 124, 130
  Japan Self-Defense Forces (JSDF) 117, 119, 124, 129, 130
  National Defense Strategy 118
  National Security Strategy 71, 118
  proximity to Taiwan 25, 66, 67, 71, 118, 126

K

Kim Jong-un 38
Kishida Fumio 12, 62, 116, 118, 129
Kissinger, Henry 23, 25
Koizumi Junichiro 61, 62
Komeito 120, 121
Korean War 33, 59, 66, 154
Kuma Academy 92
Kuomintang (KMT) 26, 27, 31, 75, 79, 80, 81, 87, 101

L

Lai Ching-te 24, 82, 84, 90, 91, 95, 97, 101
Lai, William *see* Lai Ching-te
Latin America 33, 53
Liberal Democratic Party (LDP) 118, 120, 131
Los Angeles-class submarines 70

M

Mao Zedong 25, 31
Marcos, Ferdinand R., Jr 135, 137
maritime control 30, 33
Ma Ying-jeou 79, 101
military
  capabilities 15, 53, 54, 56, 57, 61, 85, 117
  capacities 66
  equipment 30, 32, 38, 42, 43, 71
  manoeuvres 25, 39, 44, 68, 71, 99, 100
  production 39, 40
  readiness 40, 46, 47, 71, 79, 85, 87, 88, 91, 92, 96
minimal deterrence 107
missiles 67, 70, 71, 72, 86, 88, 104, 105, 106, 109, 160
Moldova 43
Mongolia, Republic of 27
Morrison, Scott 138, 141
MQ-9 *Reaper* uninhabited aerial vehicles 69, 70

N

Nakasone Yasuhiro 118
narrative about strategy 43, 45, 46, 47, 48, 49, 53, 57, 58, 62, 63, 64, 65, 72, 73, 75, 76, 77, 86, 93, 95, 96, 99, 103, 104, 110, 117, 120, 141
Narwhal submarine 89
NATO 10, 13, 15, 21, 44, 45, 48, 117, 118, 130, 134, 142, 143, 144
Naval Group 138
Netherlands, the 26, 142
New Taiwan Dollar 94
New Zealand 134
nine-dash line 31, 146
Nippon Ishin no Kai 120, 121
Nixon, Richard 23, 25
Non-Aligned Movement 53
North Korea 11, 20, 38, 61, 66, 90, 123, 124, 143

Nuclear Non-Proliferation Treaty 159
nuclear weapons 11, 13, 16, 22, *108*
   China arsenal 15, 46, 103, 106, 107, 157
   proliferation 67, 109
   Russia arsenal 10, 13, 43, 53, 54, 108, *108*
   tactical 109, 110
   US arsenal 11, 51, 53, 67, 103, 108, *108*, 157

O

Obama, Barack 61, 62, 136, 140, 142, 160
Okinawa 28, 67, 68, 69, 71, 72, 104, 118, 126
One China policy 22, 47, 56, 65, 73, 77, 101, 131
one country, two systems policy 102, 103
opinion polls 82, 84, 122

P

Pacific Ocean 31, 35, 75, 104, 111, 131, 154
Patriot surface-to-air missiles 88, 121
Pearl Harbor 41
Pelosi, Nancy 99
Philippines, the 15, 28, 30, 31, 66, 67, 71, 73, 113, 116, 134, 147, 149, 150
   Bilateral Defense Guidelines 136, 137
   defence capacity 57, 71, 116
   Mutual Defense Treaty 135
Poland 42
political will 57, 65, 85, 117, 120, 156
Pompeo, Mike 63, 64, 136
Portugal 26
Pottinger, Matt 61
propaganda 104 *see* also narrative about strategy
protests 80, 81, 122
   Sunflower Movement 80, 81, 82

psychology in conflicts 25, 40, 45, 55, 65, 66, 110, 143, 154
Putin, Vladimir 10, 20, 23, 38, 39, 40, 41, 44, 45, 110, 156

Q

Qing Dynasty 27
Quadrilateral Security Dialogue (Quad) 62, 116, 134

R

Reciprocal Access Agreements 131
Regional Comprehensive Economic Partnership 148
Rudd, Kevin 34
Russia 44
   and China 11, 57
   and NATO 44
   Joint Statement with China 11, 22, 33, 37
   nuclear weapons 21

S

sanctions 38, 39, 49
San Diego 86
Science of Military Strategy 29
second island chain 29, 30
Second World War 39, 46, 53, 73
semiconductors 38, 61, 64, 73, 74, 94
Shen, Puma 92, 93
Singapore 142, 145, 147
Sino-Japanese wars 26, 27, 73
social media 93
South China Sea 28, 30, 31, 47, 70, 73, 74, 101, 110, 111, 136, 137, 142, 145, 147
Southeast Asia 47
South Korea 31, 66, 67, 71, 72, 88, 90, 91, 104, 115, 116, 134, 142, 143
Soviet Union 20, 33, 51, 53, 59, 154
   See also Russia
Spain 26
strategic ambiguity 22, 100

Strategic Arms Limitation Treaty 159
Submarine Rotational Force–West 70, 140
submarines 67, 70, 86, 89, 90, 104, 105, 106, 116

T

Taiwan 11, 16
  as central to US–China contest 55, 102, 110, 162
  as disturbance to status quo 12, 23, 55, 83, 86, 95, 101
  as local issue 21, 23, 46, 55, 105, 155, 161
  defence spending 15, 82, 86, 88, 89, 90, 96
  democracy 26, 47, 73, 74, 83
  independence 15, 22, 56, 63, 83, 83, 95, 100, 160
  invasion of Taiwan 22, 23, 25, 38, 42, 45, 46, 47, 48, 65, 68, 69, 72, 79, 82, 85, 88, 99, 101, 103, 104, 105, 111
  Ministry of Digital Affairs 93
  Ministry of Economic Affairs 94
  unification 27, 56, 77, 82, 83, 83, 84, 99, 100, 101, 102
Taiwan Affairs Office (China) 102
Taiwan People's Party 82
Taiwan Semiconductor Manufacturing Company 74
Taiwan Strait 22, 24, 67, 75, 76, 79, 81, 82, 84, 85, 101, 102, 124
Taylor, Brendan 12, 17
technology 61, 65, 73, 74, 93, 111, 116
ten-dash line 32
Thailand 134
third world war, danger of 9, 21, 105
Tomahawk land-attack cruise missiles (LACM) 70, 71, 124
trade 17, 32, 33, 38, 39, 54, 60, 64, 73, 80, 95, 133, 141, 157
Trans-Pacific Partnership (TPP) 142
Treaty of Shimonoseki 27

Trump, Donald 42, 61, 63, 111, 142
Tsai Ing-wen 24, 85, 88, 97, 100, 101, 111
  New Southbound Policy 95
Tsao, Robert 92
Turnbull, Malcolm 138

U

Ukraine 10, 12, 13, 15, 21, 23, 33, 36, 37, 39, 41, 43, 44, 45, 47, 48, 52, 54, 66, 75, 79, 87, 88, 96, 105, 110, 112, 122
uninhabited undersea vessels 106
United Kingdom 15, 27, 70, 93, 116, 119, 131, 134, 142
  Foreign, Commonwealth and Development Office 93
United Nations 10, 33, 43, 75, 95
  UN Convention on the Law of the Sea (UNCLOS) 137, 146, 147
United States 9
  and China 12, 13, 20, 21, 49, 53, 63, 72, 75, 133, 154
  and Japan 71, 115, 117, 121, 124
  and Taiwan 21, 48, 63, 67, 68, 72, 75, 87
  as a revisionist power 63, 64
  as a status quo power 63, 64
  bipartisan consensus on China 60, 63, 111
  decision-making 48, 49, 51, 57, 63, 65, 66, 85, 87, 115
  Democratic Party 60
  Department of Defense 68, 88, 100, 106
  Indo-Pacific strategy 108, 116
  National Defense Strategy 69
  network of allies 30, 48, 57, 61, 62, 63, 67, 70, 71, 86, 103, 106, 116, 117, 133, 142, 154
  nuclear weapons 49, 51, 106
  Republican Party 42, 60, 64
  Senate Armed Services Committee 25

Seventh Fleet 67
tariffs on China 60, 61
US Air Force 67
US–China dialogue in 1971–72 23
US Marine Corps 67, 68, 69
US Navy 41
US–China Joint Communiqués 56, 74, 75, 76, 160
US–Japan Roadmap for Realignment 72

V

Vietnam 126, 142, 143, 145, 146, 147, 148, 149, 150
Vietnam War 33, 59, 134, 135
Virginia-class submarines 68, 70

W

Westminster Foundation for Democracy 93

X

Xi Jinping 11, 26, 41, 108, 110, 156

Y

Yoon Suk-yeol 143

Z

Zelenskyy, Volodymyr 43
Zheng Chenggong 26
Zhou Enlai 25
Zhu Tingchang 28

THE ADELPHI SERIES

Lawrence Freedman &
Heather Williams

CHANGING THE NARRATIVE

Information Campaigns, Strategy and Crisis Escalation in the Digital Age

Adelphi 493–495
published September 2023;
234x156; 164pp;
Paperback: 978-1-032-70786-0
eBook: 978-1-032-70787-7

available at
amazon

OR

Routledge
Taylor & Francis Group

Adelphi 496–497
published November 2023;
234x156; 200pp;
Paperback: 978-1-032-73477-4
eBook: 978-1-003-46441-9

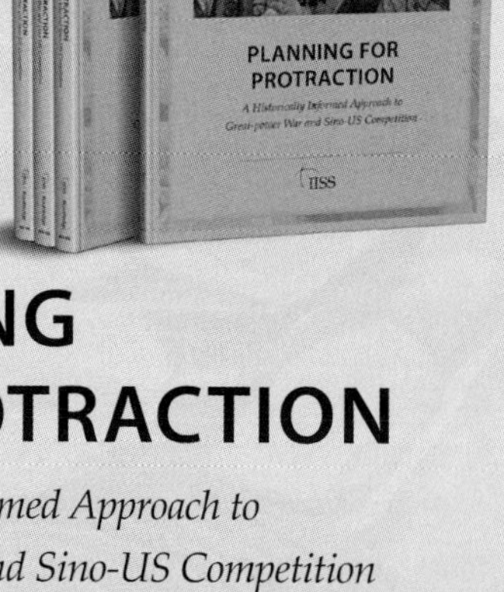

Iskander Rehman

PLANNING FOR PROTRACTION

A Historically Informed Approach to Great-power War and Sino-US Competition

IISS
THE INTERNATIONAL INSTITUTE
FOR STRATEGIC STUDIES

www.iiss.org/publications/adelphi

THE ADELPHI SERIES

THE TAMING OF SCARCITY AND THE PROBLEMS OF PLENTY

Rethinking International Relations and American Grand Strategy in a New Era

'Francis J. Gavin has created a powerful framework for understanding the radical shift in the fundamental nature of the problems the world is confronting; generating new assumptions, strategies and policy tools; and transforming local, national and global institutions. The problems of plenty demand nothing less.'

ANNE-MARIE SLAUGHTER, CEO, New America; former Director of Policy Planning, US Department of State (2009–11)

Francis J. Gavin

IISS
THE INTERNATIONAL INSTITUTE
FOR STRATEGIC STUDIES

available at
amazon
OR
Routledge
Taylor & Francis Group

Adelphi 502–504
published March 2024;
234x156; 108pp;
Paperback: 978-1-032-80557-3
eBook: 978-1-003-49743-1

The underlying structure, incentives and costs shaping international relations, state behaviour and the nature of power are profoundly different today to how they were in the past, in ways that are widely misunderstood. World politics was historically marked by profound scarcity in resources, information and security. Several historical revolutions have largely tamed this scarcity, but have also generated new, potentially catastrophic challenges – the problems of plenty.

Francis J. Gavin argues that the institutions, practices, theories and policies that helped explain and largely tamed scarcity by generating massive prosperity, and which were sometimes used to justify punishing conquest, are often unsuitable for addressing the problems of plenty. New conceptual lenses, policies and processes, and transformed institutions will be essential for confronting and solving these problems, without undermining the expanding efforts against scarcity.

www.iiss.org/publications/adelphi

JOURNAL SUBSCRIPTION INFORMATION

Six issues per year of the *Adelphi* Series (Print ISSN 1944-5571, Online ISSN 1944-558X) are published by Taylor & Francis Group, 4 Park Square, Milton Park, Abingdon, Oxon, OX14 4RN, UK.

Send address changes to Taylor & Francis Customer Services, Informa UK Ltd., Sheepen Place, Colchester, Essex CO3 3LP, UK.

Subscription records are maintained at Taylor & Francis Group, 4 Park Square, Milton Park, Abingdon, OX14 4RN, UK.

Subscription information:
For more information and subscription rates, please see tandfonline.com/pricing/journal/tadl). Taylor & Francis journals are available in a range of different packages, designed to suit every library's needs and budget. This journal is available for institutional subscriptions with online only or print & online options. This journal may also be available as part of our libraries, subject collections, or archives. For more information on our sales packages, please visit: librarianresources.taylorandfrancis.com.

For support with any institutional subscription, please visit help.tandfonline.com or email our dedicated team at subscriptions@tandf.co.uk.

Subscriptions purchased at the personal rate are strictly for personal, non-commercial use only. The reselling of personal subscriptions is prohibited. Personal subscriptions must be purchased with a personal check, credit card, or BAC/wire transfer. Proof of personal status may be requested.

Back issues:
Please visit https://taylorandfrancis.com/journals/customer-services/ for more information on how to purchase back issues.

Ordering information:
To subscribe to the Journal, please contact: T&F Customer Services, Informa UK Ltd, Sheepen Place, Colchester, Essex, CO3 3LP, United Kingdom. Tel: +44 (0) 20 8052 2030; email: subscriptions@tandf.co.uk.

Taylor & Francis journals are priced in USD, GBP and EUR (as well as AUD and CAD for a limited number of journals). All subscriptions are charged depending on where the end customer is based. If you are unsure which rate applies to you, please contact Customer Services. All subscriptions are payable in advance and all rates include postage. We are required to charge applicable VAT/GST on all print and online combination subscriptions, in addition to our online only journals. Subscriptions are entered on an annual basis, i.e., January to December. Payment may be made by sterling check, dollar check, euro check, international money order, National Giro or credit cards (Amex, Visa and Mastercard).

Disclaimer: The International Institute for Strategic Studies and our publisher Taylor & Francis make every effort to ensure the accuracy of all the information (the "Content") contained in our publications. However, The International Institute for Strategic Studies and our publisher Taylor & Francis, our agents (including the editor, any member of the editorial team or editorial board, and any guest editors), and our licensors make no representations or warranties whatsoever as to the accuracy, completeness, or suitability for any purpose of the Content. Any opinions and views expressed in this publication are the opinions and views of the authors, and are not the views of or endorsed by The International Institute for Strategic Studies and our publisher Taylor & Francis. The accuracy of the Content should not be relied upon and should be independently verified with primary sources of information. The International Institute for Strategic Studies and our publisher Taylor & Francis shall not be liable for any losses, actions, claims, proceedings, demands, costs, expenses, damages, and other liabilities whatsoever or howsoever caused arising directly or indirectly in connection with, in relation to, or arising out of the use of the Content. Terms & Conditions of access and use can be found at http://www.tandfonline.com/page/terms-and-conditions.

All Taylor & Francis Group journals are printed on paper from renewable sources by accredited partners.